# Reach
# HIGHER

**Program Authors**

Nancy Frey

Lada Kratky

Nonie K. Lesaux

Sylvia Linan-Thompson

Deborah J. Short

Jennifer D. Turner

**NATIONAL
GEOGRAPHIC**
L E A R N I N G

Australia · Brazil · Mexico · Singapore · United Kingdom · United States

**NATIONAL
GEOGRAPHIC**
L E A R N I N G

National Geographic Learning,
a Cengage Company

**Reach Higher 1B**
**Program Authors: Nancy Frey, Lada Kratky,
Nonie K. Lesaux, Sylvia Linan-Thompson,
Deborah J. Short, Jennifer D. Turner**

Publisher, Content-based English:
  Erik Gundersen

Associate Director, R&D: Barnaby Pelter

Senior Development Editors:
  Jacqueline Eu

  Ranjini Fonseka

  Kelsey Zhang

Director of Global Marketing: Ian Martin

Heads of Regional Marketing:
  Charlotte Ellis (Europe, Middle East and Africa)

  Kiel Hamm (Asia)

  Irina Pereyra (Latin America)

Product Marketing Manager: David Spain

Senior Production Controller: Tan Jin Hock

Senior Media Researcher (Covers): Leila Hishmeh

Senior Designer: Lisa Trager

Director, Operations: Jason Seigel

Operations Support:
  Rebecca Barbush

  Drew Robertson

  Caroline Stephenson

  Nicholas Yeaton

Manufacturing Planner: Mary Beth Hennebury

Publishing Consultancy and Composition:
  MPS North America LLC

For permission to use material from this text or product,
submit all requests online at **cengage.com/permissions**
Further permissions questions can be emailed to
**permissionrequest@cengage.com**

ISBN-13: 978-0-357-36656-1

**National Geographic Learning**
200 Pier Four Blvd
Boston, MA 02210
USA

Locate your local office at **international.cengage.com/region**

Visit National Geographic Learning online at **ELTNGL.com**
Visit our corporate website at **www.cengage.com**

Printed in Mexico
Print Number: 04      Print Year: 2021

# Contents at a Glance

# Table of Contents

## Creature Features

### Unit 5

**?) BIG QUESTION**

How are animals different from one another?

Extra phonics support with **READ ON YOUR OWN**

**Around the World**

## SCIENCE
▸ **Animal Features**
▸ **Animal Movement**

**Animals Small
and Huge**

# Table of Contents

## Up in the Air

## Unit 6

Extra phonics support with **READ ON YOUR OWN**

**Weather to Remember**

## SCIENCE
▸ **Weather**
▸ **Seasons**

**Goods: From
Here to There**

# Table of Contents

## Then and Now

## Unit 7

**?** **BIG QUESTION**

What's the difference between then and now?

**Part 1**

*Extra phonics support with* **READ ON YOUR OWN**

**What a Shop!**

# SOCIAL STUDIES

▸ Past and Present
▸ Inventions and Technology

**Everyday Inventions**

**Teams Work Together**

# Table of Contents

## Get Out the Map!

## Unit 8

Extra phonics support with **READ ON YOUR OWN**

 **Watch Out!**

## SOCIAL STUDIES

‣ Maps
‣ Signs and Symbols

**Look Out!**

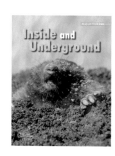

**Inside and Underground**

# Genres at a Glance

# Unit 5

# Creature Features

**?**
**BIG**
**Question**

How are animals different from one another?

JAVA, INDONESIA
A golden frog sitting on a crocodile

Unit at a Glance
▸ **Language Focus**: Compare and Contrast, Give Information
▸ **Reading Strategy**: Make Connections
▸ **Phonics Focus**: Long *u* spelled *u_e, ue*; Sounds and Spellings: *ge, gi, dge*
▸ **Topic**: Animals

## Share What You Know

Do It!

❶ **Draw** an animal.

❷ **Name** or point to different parts of your animal.

❸ **Say** or show how your animal moves.

## Compare and Contrast

Listen and chant.

# Legs

Chant

Flamingos have legs,

**And** alligators do, **too**.

Alligators have four legs,

**But** flamingos have two!

leg

# ◀)) Key Words

**Parts**

**Coverings**

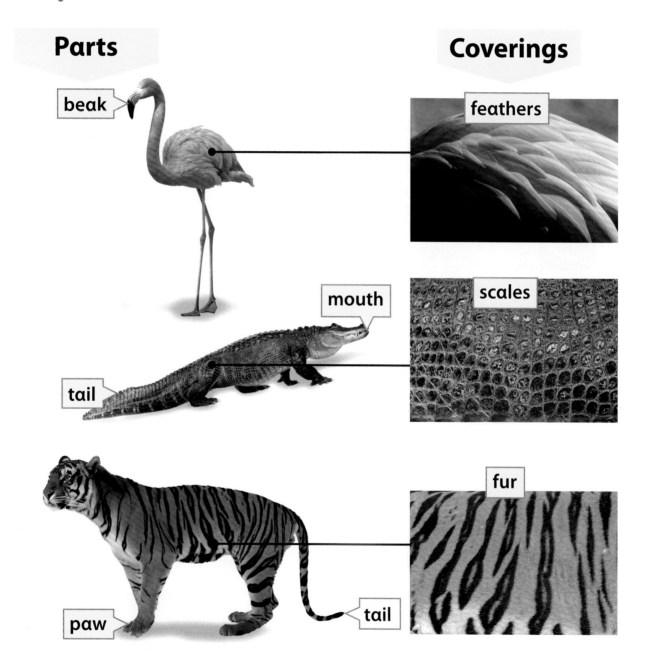

beak

feathers

mouth

scales

tail

paw

fur

tail

Look at the parts and coverings of animals on this page. How are they different?

# Compare and Contrast

**Venn Diagram**

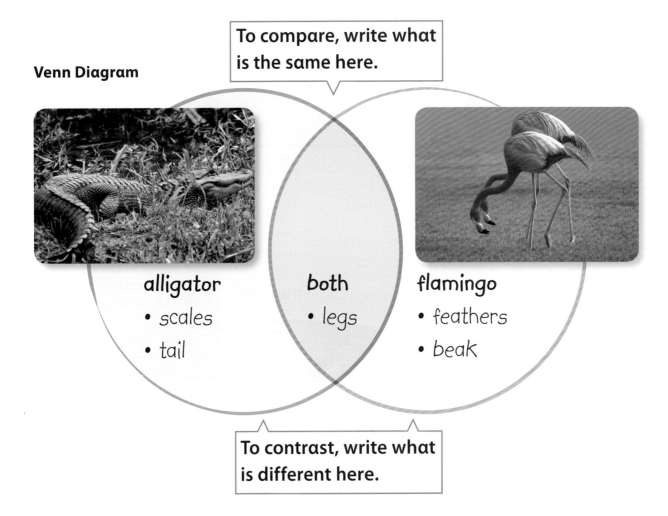

To compare, write what is the same here.

alligator
- scales
- tail

both
- legs

flamingo
- feathers
- beak

To contrast, write what is different here.

**Talk Together**

Choose two animal picture cards. Make a Venn diagram. Compare and contrast the animals.

# 🔊 More Key Words

## alike

These cats are **alike**.

## • body

A baby has a small **body**.

## different

These fruits are **different**.

## feature

neck

A long neck is the main **feature** of a giraffe.

## • look

These apples **look** the same.

**Talk Together**

Use one **Key Word** in a sentence.

> I look like my brother.

• Words to Know

# 🔊 Long *u* spelled *u_e, ue*

cube

hue

**Listen** and **Learn**

🔊 Listen to the picture words. Choose the correct word for each picture. Then write the word.

**1.**

mull   mule   mole

**2.**

full   fall   fuel

Use one of the words from above to finish each sentence.

**1.** The _____ is in the car.

**2.** The _____ can pull the cart.

Listen and read. Find the words with the long *u* sound.

## Alike and Different

What body parts do birds have? They have eyes and legs. They have wings, feathers, and a beak. Birds can be many hues, or colors, such as blue or black.

A turtle does not have wings. It does not have feathers. It has a shell. But a turtle does have eyes and legs. It has a beak, too. Turtles and birds use their beaks to eat.

Some animals look cute. Others look scary. One thing about animals is true: they are alike in some ways and different in other ways.

**Work with a partner.**
Take turns using the long *u* words from the passage in sentences of your own.

◄ Read "Alike and Different" with a partner. Practice reading the long *u* words.

9

# Read a Story

An **animal fantasy** is a story that is not true. The animals act like people.

## Characters

Characters are the people or animals in the story.

Pete

Pete's Friends

## Reading Strategy

**Make connections** as you read.

How are your feelings like Pete's feelings?

# For Pete's Sake

by **Ellen Stoll Walsh**

"I'm green," said Pete. "I want to be pink. Everyone else is."

"Don't worry," said the others. "You probably aren't ripe yet. It takes longer for some."

"Is that true?" Pete wondered.

"Probably," they said. "Let's play in the sand!"

"Oh no," cried Pete. "I have four feet. No one else has four feet."

"You're lucky, Pete," said the others.
"Two, and two extra. C'mon. Let's
go wading."

Pete tried to feel lucky.
Before long he was having fun.

"Stop!" said the others, laughing.
"You're getting our **feathers** wet."
Uh-oh. Pete didn't have any feathers.

"The best **feathers** take the longest to grow," they said. "Hurry, it's getting late."

The others hurried home.

But poor, green, featherless Pete poked along on his four feet…

very, very slowly.

Nothing could cheer him up.

Then one day some strangers
stopped by on their way to the swamp.
Flamingos who **looked** just like Pete.
Pete almost popped with joy.

"I'm **different** but the same,"
he told the others.

"Well, for Pete's sake, Pete,"
they said. "You always have been." ❖

## Meet the Author

# Ellen Stoll Walsh

**AWARD WINNER**

Ellen Stoll Walsh has nine brothers and sisters. Ellen was the family storyteller.

Ellen grew up and started writing stories to read to her children. Now she can't imagine doing anything else!

**Writing Tip**

Find words that Ellen Stoll Walsh used to show what Pete and his friends look like. Can you add some words?

## Talk About It

**1.** What do Pete and his friends do together?

Pete and his friends _____ .

**2.** What does Pete want? Why?

Pete wants _____ . He _____ .

**3.** How can you tell that Pete's friends like him the way he is? Explain.

I can tell Pete's friends like him because _____ .

## Write About It

Make connections. How are your friends like Pete's friends? How are they **different**?

Pete's friends _____ , and my friends _____ , too.
Pete's friends _____ , but my friends _____ .

# Compare Characters

How are the characters **different** ?

How are they **alike** ?

**Venn Diagram**

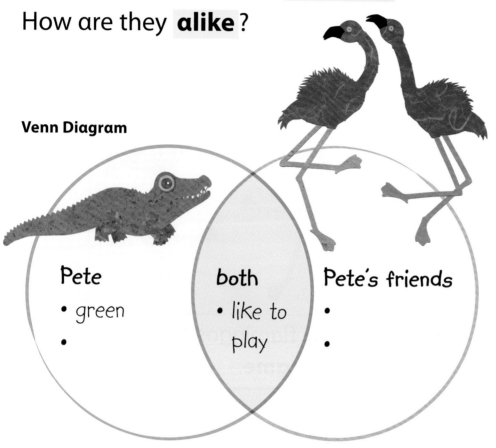

Pete
• green
•

both
• like to play

Pete's friends
•
•

Use your diagram. Tell a partner about Pete and Pete's friends.

Pete's friends have **feathers** .

33

# Synonyms

| alike | same |
|---|---|
| The flamingos are **alike**. | The flamingos are the **same**. |

**Alike** and **same** are **synonyms**. They have the same meaning.

**Try It Together**

Talk about these pairs of words. Are they synonyms? Why or why not?

| object | thing |
|---|---|
| sick | happy |
| bad | paw |
| quickly | fast |

**Making Connections** Learn more about what makes alligators **different**.

**Genre** A **science article** is nonfiction. This article gives information about alligators.

# ALLIGATORS

by Julie Larson

# An Alligator Home

Many alligators live in the Florida Everglades. The Everglades has many rivers and islands.

The Everglades

Tallahassee ⊛
Jacksonville
**FLORIDA**
Gulf of Mexico
Tampa •
Miami •
*EVERGLADES*

How do alligators' **bodies** help them live in the Everglades? Let's find out.

## Alligator Bodies

Alligators have short legs. They can hide in tall grass. They can also hide under the water. Sometimes, you can only see their eyes. Can you see the alligator?

37

tail

## Alligator Tails

Alligator **tails** can be more than 5 feet long. This is probably taller than you! Tails help alligators swim and move through the mud.

leg

**Tails** help alligators leap up to catch food.
Alligators can leap 5 feet into the air! ❖

# Compare Genres

How are "For Pete's Sake" and "Alligators" different?

**Animal Fantasy**

Then one day some strangers stopped by on their way to the swamp. Flamingos who **looked** just like Pete. Pete almost popped with joy.

**Animals don't really have feelings.**

28 Unit 5

**Science Article**

**An Alligator Home**
Many alligators live in the Florida Everglades. The Everglades has many rivers and islands.

**Sentences give information.**

*Gulf of Mexico* Tampa
Miami
*EVERGLADES*

How do alligators' **bodies** help them live in the Everglades? Let's find out.

36 Unit 5

**Talk Together**

Think about what you read and learned. How are animals **different**?

# Complete Sentences

**A sentence tells a complete thought.**

An alligator's tail 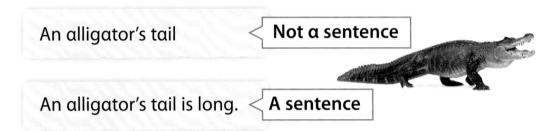 **Not a sentence**

An alligator's tail is long. **A sentence**

## Grammar Rules Complete Sentences

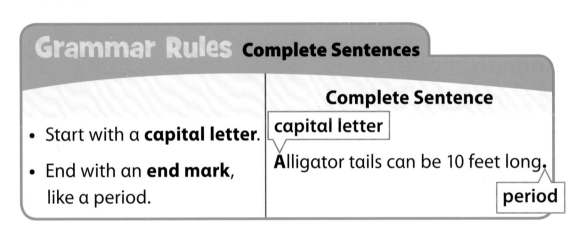

**Complete Sentence**

- Start with a **capital letter**.

- End with an **end mark**, like a period.

capital letter

**A**lligator tails can be 10 feet long.

period

## Read a Sentence

Which group of words is a sentence?

How do you know?

1. leap up
2. Tails help alligators leap up to catch food.

## Write a Sentence

Write a sentence about alligators. Read it to a partner.

Words to
Know

is

this

use

## Give Information

Listen and chant.

**Chant**

# How Do They Move?

Animals move.
Yes, they do.
How do they go?
Do you know?

This is a fish.
A fish swims.
A fish uses fins to
move in water!

Fish swim.
Yes, they do.
How do they go?
Now you know!

## ◀» Key Words

How do animals move?

**swim**

A fish swims.

**fly**

A bird flies.

**run**

A polar bear runs.

**climb**

A monkey climbs.

**slide**

A penguin slides.

**slither**

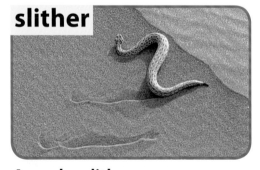

A snake slithers.

**Talk Together**

Act out how animals move. How are animals different?

# Categorize Details

**Category Chart**

| Animals | Movement |
|---|---|
| fish<br>turtle | swim |
| | fly |
| | run |
| | |
| | |
| | |

Write the big ideas here.

Write the details here.

**Talk** **Together**

Sort picture cards. Add animals to the Category Chart. Act out how the animals move. How are they different?

## 🔊 More Key Words

### • back

The **back** tire is flat.

### fact

It's a **fact** that a dog has four legs.

### front

The **front** of the house is blue.

### movement

The **movement** of a turtle is slow.

### push

We had to **push** the car.

**Talk Together**

Use a **Key Word** to ask a question about animals.

What is one fact about turtles?

• Words to Know

# 🔊 Sounds and Spellings: *ge, gi, dge*

cage

giant

bridge

**Listen** and **Learn**

🔊 Listen to each word. Sort the words by which spelling is used.

| page | giant | edge | fudge | age | giraffe |
|------|-------|------|-------|-----|---------|

**ge**                    **gi**                    **dge**

_____      _____      _____

_____      _____      _____

Choose two words from above. Write your own sentences with the words.

🔊 Listen and read. Find the words with the sound you hear at the beginning of the word *jet* spelled *ge*, *gi*, or *dge*.

## Moving Along

How do animals move? Fish swim. Birds fly. Snakes slither. Monkeys climb high in the trees. Animals like giraffes run fast.

How do you move? Can you run like a giraffe? Can you walk slowly like a turtle? Can you climb a huge slide? Then do you slither down? Can you jump over a hedge? Can you take huge steps like a giant in a story? It is good to move and use your body. This helps keep you healthy and strong.

**Work with a partner.**
Point to a word in the passage with the sound you hear at the beginning of the word *giant*. Have your partner say it and tell how the sound is spelled.

◀ Read "Moving Along" with a partner. Practice reading the words with the sound you hear at the beginning of the word *giant*.

# Read a Fact Book

A **fact book** is nonfiction. It gives facts about things that are real.

✓ Look for labels.

## Reading Strategy

**Make connections** as you read. Connect new facts to things you have read in other texts and to things you know about the world.

# Slither, Slide, Hop, and Run

by Katharine Kenah

# Fly

feathers

wing

A bird can **fly**! It moves through the air with wings.

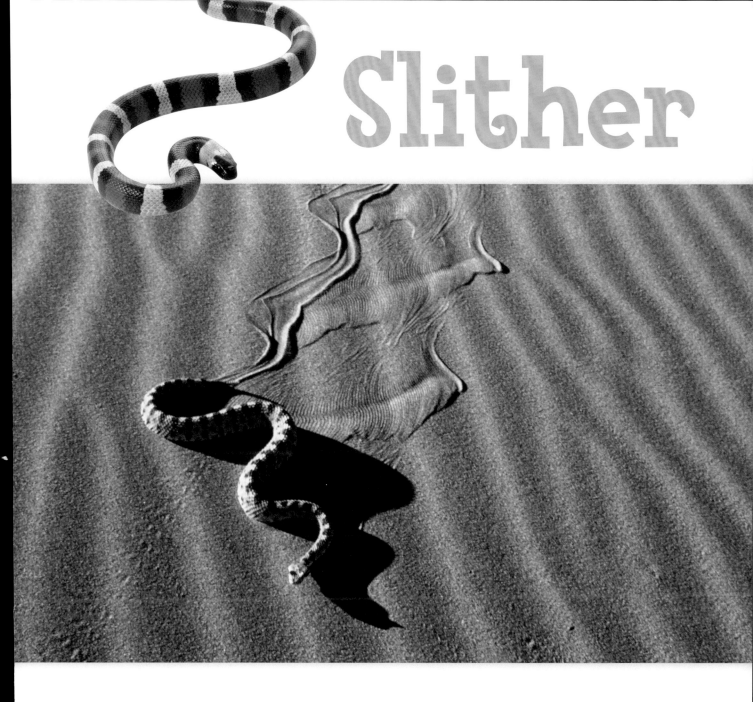

# Slither

A snake can **slither**! It wiggles from side to side on the ground.

# Hop

back feet

A kangaroo can hop! It makes short leaps into the air. It uses its **back** feet to hop.

# Run

leg

A horse can **run**! Its legs move forward
and backward very quickly.

# Slide

hard shell

soft body

A snail can **slide**! It moves slowly along the ground. A snail has a soft body inside its hard shell.

# Crawl

leg

A spider can crawl! It creeps forward
with its legs.

# Hang

claws

A sloth can hang! It holds onto a tree and hangs below it. A sloth has long claws.

# Swim

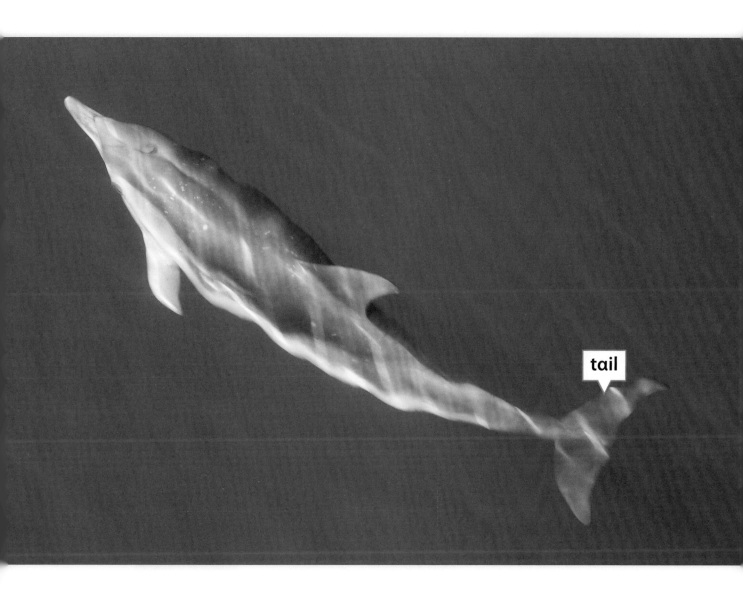

tail

A dolphin can **swim**! It moves gently through the water. A dolphin swims by moving its tail up and down.

# Glide

wing

A bat can glide! It flies smoothly through the air. A bat's wings are really long fingers covered with skin.

# Dig

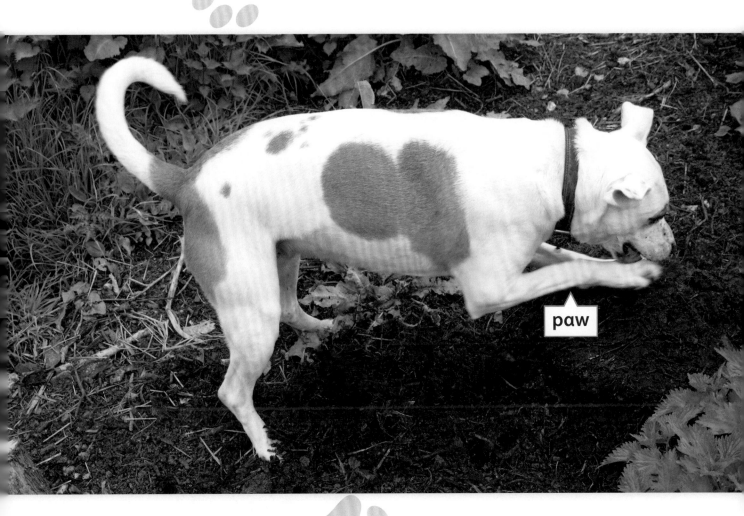

paw

A dog can dig! It uses its paws to
move dirt.

# Climb

front foot

back foot

A raccoon can **climb**! It moves up and down by using its feet. Its **front** and **back** feet work like hands.

# Waddle

A penguin can waddle! It rocks from side to side as it walks. A penguin can waddle as fast as a person walks! ❖

# Talk About It

1. What does the **fact** book tell you about animals?

   The fact book tells _____.

2. Name two animals in the book that slide on the ground.

   _____ and _____ **slide** on the ground.

3. How do other books you have read help you understand this fact book?

   Other books help me _____.

# Write About It

What is interesting about how animals move? Write one sentence.

It is interesting that ____ .

# Categorize Details

How do animals move?

**Category Chart**

| Animals | Movement |
|---|---|
| birds<br>bats | fly |
| horses | |
| | |
| | |
| | |

Use your chart to summarize what you learned in "Slither, Slide, Hop, and Run."

# Antonyms

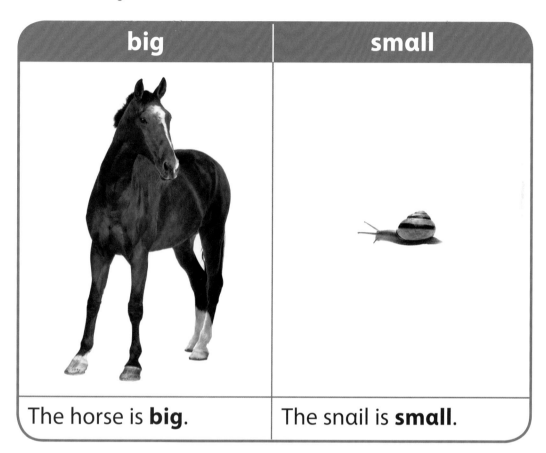

| big | small |
|---|---|
| The horse is **big**. | The snail is **small**. |

**Big** and **small** have opposite meanings. Words with opposite meanings are called **antonyms**.

**Try It Together**

Choose animal picture cards. Use the antonyms to compare the animals.

| Antonyms | |
|---|---|
| big | small |
| fast | slow |
| front | back |
| hard | soft |

NATIONAL
GEOGRAPHIC
EXCLUSIVE

**Making Connections** Read about a camera that films animals moving in different ways.

**Genre** A **photo journal** shows something important in a person's life. It uses words and photos.

# My Crittercam Journal

## by Greg Marshall

July 8

camera
body

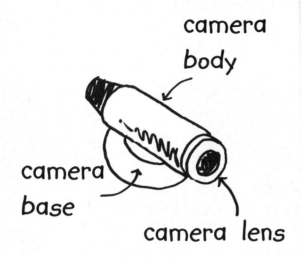

camera
base

camera lens

Here's the camera my team and I made.
I call it Crittercam.

July 10

Today we put Crittercam on a whale.
I saw how it eats and swims.

August 20

I'm in Africa! Today Crittercam filmed a lion's movements. It runs fast!

August 21

Today I watched my Crittercam videos. The penguin video was really exciting. ❖

# Compare Genres

How are "Slither, Slide, Hop, and Run" and "My Crittercam Journal" alike and different?

**Fact Book**

**Photo Journal**

**Talk Together**

Think about what you read and learned. How do animals use their bodies to **push**, pull, and move?

# Subject-Verb Agreement

In a sentence, the **subject** and the **verb** go together.

One **frog** **hops**.

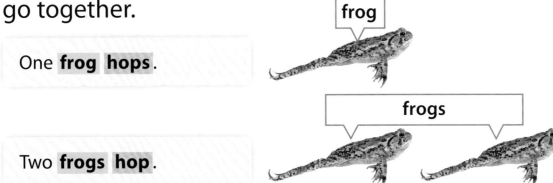

frog

frogs

Two **frogs** **hop**.

| **Grammar Rules** Subject-Verb Agreement | |
| --- | --- |
| | **Subject-Verb Agreement** |
| If the **subject** names one, use <u>s</u> at the end of the **verb**. | If the **subject** names more than one, do not use <u>s</u> at the end of the **verb**. |

## Read a Sentence

Why does the verb below have <u>s</u>?

A dolphin swims in the ocean.

## Write a Sentence

Write a sentence about how an animal moves.
Read it to a partner.

# Write Like a Scientist

## Write an Article ✏️

What do you know about animals? Describe an animal. Write an article for your classmates.

Penguins

by Roberto Garcia

main idea ▷ A penguin is a special bird. Most birds have wings. Most birds use their wings to fly.

details ▷ A penguin has wings. But it doesn't fly! Penguins use their wings to swim under water.

An article gives information about a topic.

The main idea of my article is _____.

## ① Plan and Write

Talk about animals with a partner. Pick an animal. Discuss your plan. Draw your animal and write a list of details. Tell your partner your main idea.

Write your main idea. Then write sentences with details.

## ② Check Your Work

Revise and edit your writing. Use this checklist.

### Checklist

☑ Think about different words you can use. Can you use synonyms?

☑ Check your sentences. Did you use the right end mark?

☑ Trade work with a partner. Check the spelling. Correct spelling errors.

## ③ Finish and Share

Finish your drawing. Write each sentence neatly. Make sure you leave enough space between each sentence.

Read your article aloud. Listen to your partner's article. Share what you know.

I know that peguins can't fly.

71

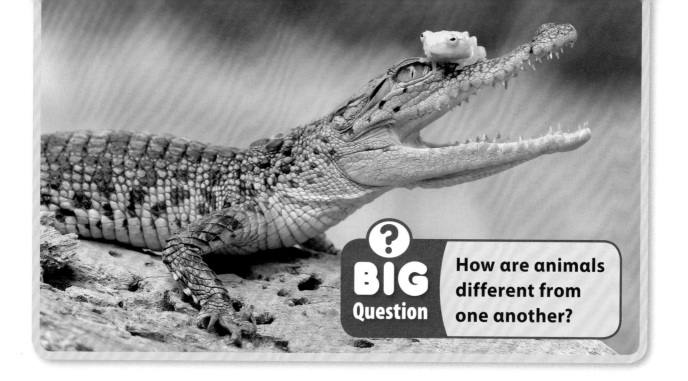

**BIG Question**

How are animals different from one another?

# Share Your Ideas

Think about how animals move and look. How are animals different? Choose one of these ways to share your ideas about the **Big Question**.

## Write It!

### Draw and Label
Draw your favorite animal from the unit. Label the animal's parts. Write a sentence about your animal.

tail

legs    teeth

Alligators have four legs.

# Talk About It!

**Interview**

Have an interview with a partner. The **reporter** asks questions about how animals look and move. The **expert** answers the questions.

How do penguins move?

They waddle!

**Reporter**

**Expert**

# Do It!

**I Am an Animal**

Pretend you are an animal. Make a mask. In a group, act out how your animal moves.

# Up in the Air

## BIG Question

**What's wild about weather?**

WESTERN KANSAS, USA
**Professional storm chasers monitoring
an approaching tornado**

**Unit at a Glance**
▷ **Language Focus**: Explain, Express Ideas
▷ **Reading Strategy**: Make Inferences
▷ **Phonics Focus**: Sounds and Spellings:
  *ce, ci, ch, tch, wh*
▷ **Topic**: Weather

## Share What You Know

*Do It!*

❶ **Name** your favorite kind of weather.

❷ **Tell** why you like that weather.

❸ **Draw** something you do in that weather.

## Explain

Listen and sing.

**Song**

# *Wind*

The wind is made of air.

The wind is made of air.

Let me explain it one more time

How wind is made of air.

Wind can blow trees down.

And blow your hat around.

Let me explain it one more time

How wind can blow trees down.

Tune: "The Farmer in the Dell"

## ◀)) Key Words

What happens when the **wind** **blows**?

storm

**Weather** changes.

It can make electricity.

Things move.

It **feels** good.

**Talk Together**

Look at the windy weather. Explain what different kinds of wind can do. What is wild about wind?

# Find Cause and Effect

**Cause-and-Effect Chart**

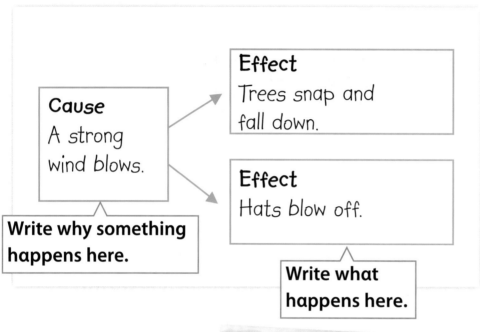

**Cause**
A strong wind blows.

**Effect**
Trees snap and fall down.

**Effect**
Hats blow off.

Write why something happens here.

Write what happens here.

**Talk Together**

Talk to a partner about rain. Explain what happens when it rains. Make a cause-and-effect chart.

## 🔊 More Key Words

### fast

This car goes **fast**.

### outside

They run **outside**.

### power

This toaster uses **power**.

### soft

pillow

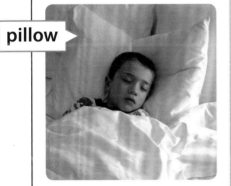

Pillows are **soft**.

### strong

We are **strong**.

**Talk Together**

Sort the **Key Words** by syllables.

Fast has one syllable.

Outside has two syllables.

# 🔊 Sounds and Spellings: *ce, ci*

fen**ce**

**ci**rcus

**Listen** and **Learn**

🔊 Listen to each group of words. Choose the word with the sound you hear at the beginning of the word *see*.

**1.** city          kitty          pity

**2.** vent          dent          cent

**3.** pride         price         prime

**4.** ate           aid           ace

🔊 Listen and read. Find the words with the *s* sound spelled with the letters *ce* or *ci*.

## A Huge Rainstorm

The wind begins to blow harder and harder. The clouds look dark and angry. A storm can come fast. People race to bring their pets inside. The power might go out. People look for candles. They decide to stay away from windows. They find a safe place.

The rain comes. It fills the city streets. Strong winds bend the trees. Then, slowly, the clouds move on. The wind stops blowing. The wind made a mess, but it is quiet once the storm has gone.

**Work with a partner.**
Find the words with the sound you hear at the beginning of the word *see*. Take turns using the words in sentences.

◄ Read "A Huge Rainstorm" with a partner. Practice reading words with the sound you hear at the beginning of the word *see*.

# Read Science Nonfiction

**Science nonfiction** gives information about a science topic, like weather.

✓ Look for illustrations. Illustrations are drawings that show information.

illustration

## Reading Strategy

**Make inferences** as you read. Use what you know and details from the text to make inferences about what wind does.

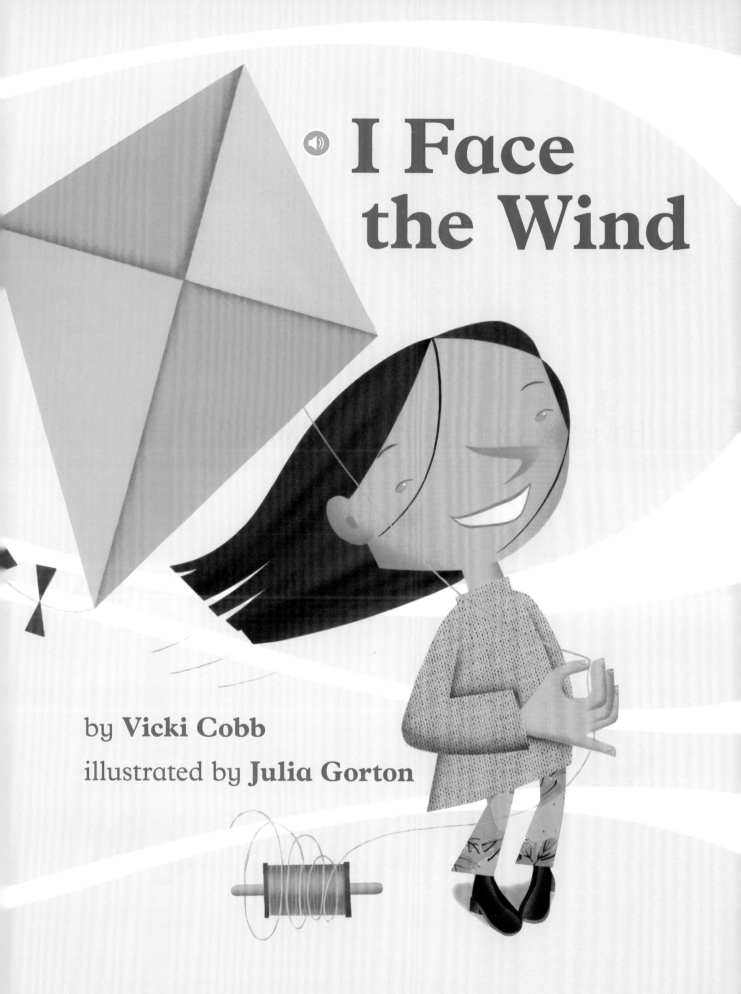

# I Face the Wind

by **Vicki Cobb**

illustrated by **Julia Gorton**

Have you ever felt a **strong** **wind**?

Your hair **blows** away from your face. You could lose your hat. You may even have to walk at a slant.

You can't see the **wind**. But you can **feel** it. And you can see what **wind** does to other things.

It makes flags stick out straight and flutter.

Can you name some things you see **wind** do?

Go **outside** and watch.

Leaves on trees shake.

A kite stays in the sky.

An umbrella turns inside out.

What is **wind** made of?

Wind is made of air. You can't see air. But you can catch it. Here's how:

1 Open a large plastic bag.
Make sure there are no holes in it.

2 Pull the bag through the air so it puffs up.

**3** Twist it closed to trap the air you caught.

**4** Squeeze the bag to **feel** the air.

Are there other ways you can make **wind**?

**Blow** air out of your mouth. Wave your hand in front of your face. Be an inventor and make your own kind of air movers.

The **fastest winds** of all are in a tornado. These winds are so **strong** they can lift a roof right off a house!

One of the **softest** **winds** is your breath. Put your fingertips near your nose. **Feel** your soft breath.

Face the **wind**. **Feel** the push of the wind. Yay! ❖

# Talk About It

1.  What is **wind** made of?

    Wind is made of _____ .

2.  What happens when the wind **blows**?

    When the wind blows, _____
    will _____ .

3.  Why might you have to walk at a slant when
    a **strong** wind blows?

    You might have to walk at a slant because
    _____ .

# Write About It

Use the illustrations and steps on pages 92
and 93. Retell how to catch air.

You can catch air _____ .

# Find Cause and Effect

The **wind** **blows** . This is the cause.
What are the effects?

**Cause-and-Effect Chart**

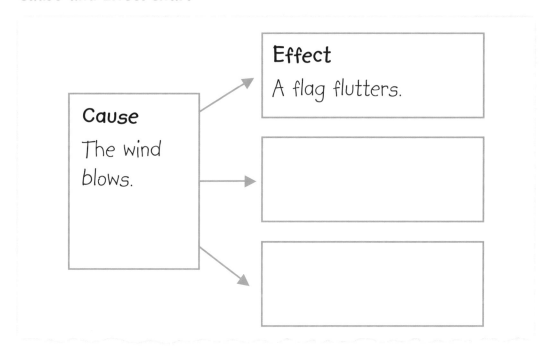

Use your cause-and-effect chart. Tell a partner
facts you learned in "I Face the Wind."

# Compound Words

Touch your nose with your fingertips.

**finger + tips = fingertips** ‹ compound word

Learn the meanings of both words to understand the **compound word**.

**finger**      • We have five **fingers** on each hand.

**+ tips**      • **Tips** mean ends.

**fingertips**  • **Fingertips** are the ends of fingers.

**Try It Together**

Talk about the meaning of each compound word. Use the two shorter words to help you. Then draw a picture to show the compound word. Label your drawing.

| rain | + | coat | = | raincoat |
| snow | + | glasses | = | sunglasses |
| snow | + | man | = | snowman |

**Making Connections** Learn more about how the **wind** can be wild and gentle.

**Genre** A **legend** is a story from long ago. This legend explains why the wind **blows** in different ways.

# Wind Eagle

## A Native American legend

retold by **Renee Biermann**

illustrations by **Amanda Hall**

Gluscabi could not fish. There was too much **wind**. The wind pushed his boat. He went to see Wind Eagle. Wind Eagle was making too much wind!

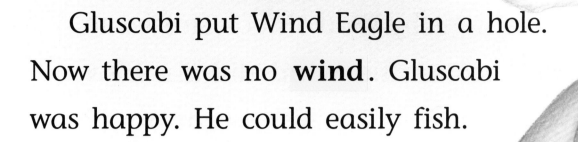

Gluscabi put Wind Eagle in a hole.
Now there was no **wind**. Gluscabi
was happy. He could easily fish.

Weeks went by. Bad things started to happen because the **wind** did not **blow**. Everyone was hot. The fish began to die. The people in the village were not happy.

Gluscabi went to see Wind Eagle. Wind Eagle promised to make gentle **winds**. So Gluscabi took Wind Eagle out of the hole.

But on some days Wind Eagle forgets his promise. That's why some days **feel** very windy. ❖

# Character's Action

In "Wind Eagle," what are the reasons for Gluscabi's actions?

| Gluscabi's Actions | Reasons |
|---|---|
| Gluscabi went to see Wind Eagle. | There was too much wind. Gluscabi couldn't fish. |
| Gluscabi put Wind Eagle in a hole. | |
| Gluscabi went to see Wind Eagle again. | |
| Gluscabi took Wind Eagle out of the hole. | |

**Talk Together**

Think about what you read and learned. What's wild about **weather** ?

# Sentence Types

There are four **types of sentences**.

| **Grammar Rules** Sentence Types | |
|---|---|
| 1. A **statement** tells something. It ends with a **period**. | • Gluscabi could not fish. <br> period |
| 2. A **question** asks something. It ends with a **question mark**. | • Can you feel the wind? <br> question mark |
| 3. An **exclamation** shows strong feeling. It ends with an **exclamation point**. | • There is too much wind! <br> exclamation point |
| 4. A **command** tells someone to do something. It starts with a verb. It ends with a **period** or an **exclamation point**. | • Stop, Wind Eagle! <br> exclamation point |

## Read a Sentence

What types of sentences are these? How do you know?

It was so hot!

The fish began to die.

## Write a Sentence

Write a sentence about today's weather.
Read it aloud.

## Express Ideas

Listen and sing.

**Song**

# Watching the Weather

I **see** big, dark clouds today.

I **think that** we will get rain.

I see a bright sun outside.

I think we'll be hot tonight!

I see snow fall from the sky.

I think we'll have a snowball fight!

Tune: "Twinkle Twinkle, Little Star"

## 🔊 Key Words

What is the weather?

snowy

rainy

Weather

sunny

cloudy

The weather is different
every **month** of the **year**.

calendar

What is the weather like today? Is it wild?

# Classify Details

**Classification Chart**

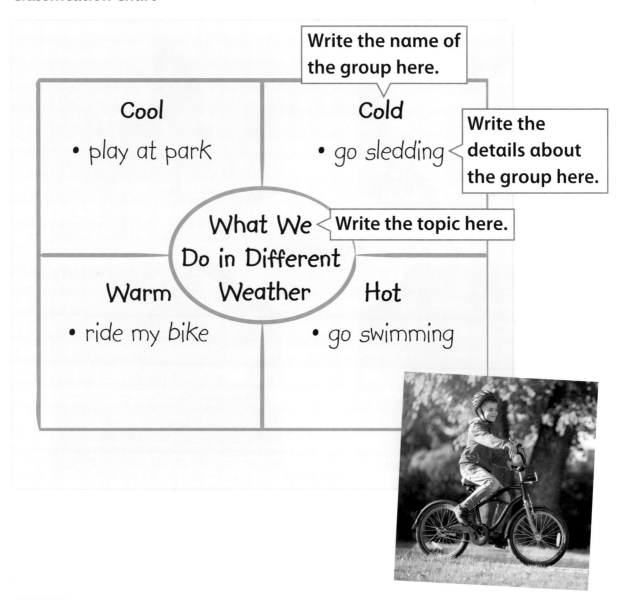

Write the name of the group here.

Cool
• play at park

Cold
• go sledding

Write the details about the group here.

What We Do in Different Weather ◁ Write the topic here.

Warm
• ride my bike

Hot
• go swimming

**Talk Together**

Tell your partner what you do in different kinds of weather. Add to the classification chart. How is your weather wild?

## 🔊 More Key Words

**cold**

It's **cold** today.

**cool**

The fan keeps me **cool**.

**hot**

The stove is **hot**.

**temperature**

The **temperature** is 8° Fahrenheit.

**warm**

The blanket keeps us **warm**.

**Talk Together**

Ask a question using a **Key Word**.

What do you wear when it is cold outside?

# 🔊 Sounds and Spellings: *ch, tch, wh*

chair

watch

wheel

**Listen and Learn**

🔊 Listen to the picture words. Write the correct letters to complete each word.

**1.**

__ __ eese

**2.**

pi __ __ __

**3.**

__ __ ale

**4.**

__ __ imp

🔊 Listen and read. Find the words with *ch*, *tch*, or *wh* in the story.

**Over to You**

### Sunny or Rainy?

"What is it like outside?" asked Chico.

Sancho checked. "It's sunny," he said. "I think it's warm but not hot."

"Great! Let's play ball," said Chico.

The boys went out to play. They pitched the ball back and forth. They did not see the sky get cloudy. The temperature got cool. The sunny day changed to a rainy day.

The boys raced home.

"What can we do now?" asked Chico.

"We could play checkers," said Sancho. "That is a good game for a rainy day."

**Work with a partner.**
Take turns. Find a word with the spellings *ch*, *tch*, or *wh*. Say the word. Have your partner find it in the passage and read the sentence.

◀ Read "Sunny or Rainy?" with a partner. Practice reading words with the spellings *ch*, *tch*, and *wh*.

# Read Realistic Fiction

**Realistic fiction** is a story that is made up, but could happen in real life.

## Sensory Details

Sensory details tell what characters see, hear, smell, taste, and touch.

sensory detail

February is cold and still.

## Reading Strategy

**Make inferences** as you read. How do you think Kiko feels about the different weather?

# A Year for Kiko

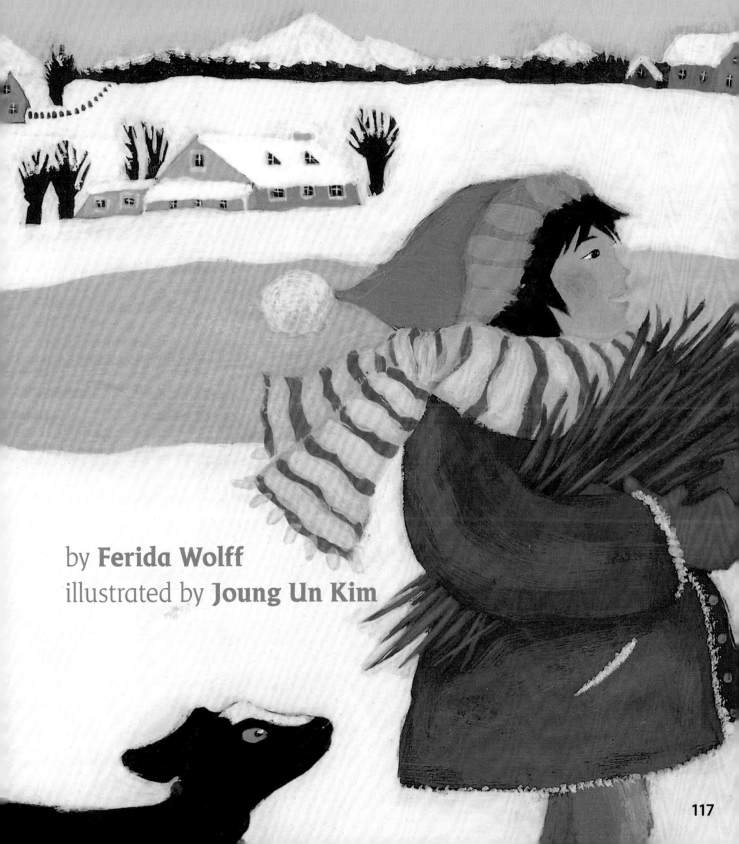

by **Ferida Wolff**
illustrated by **Joung Un Kim**

January snow is falling.

Kiko slips in the snow.

February is **cold** and still.
Kiko's window is frosted white.
Kiko draws a smile with her
finger. The smile melts the ice.

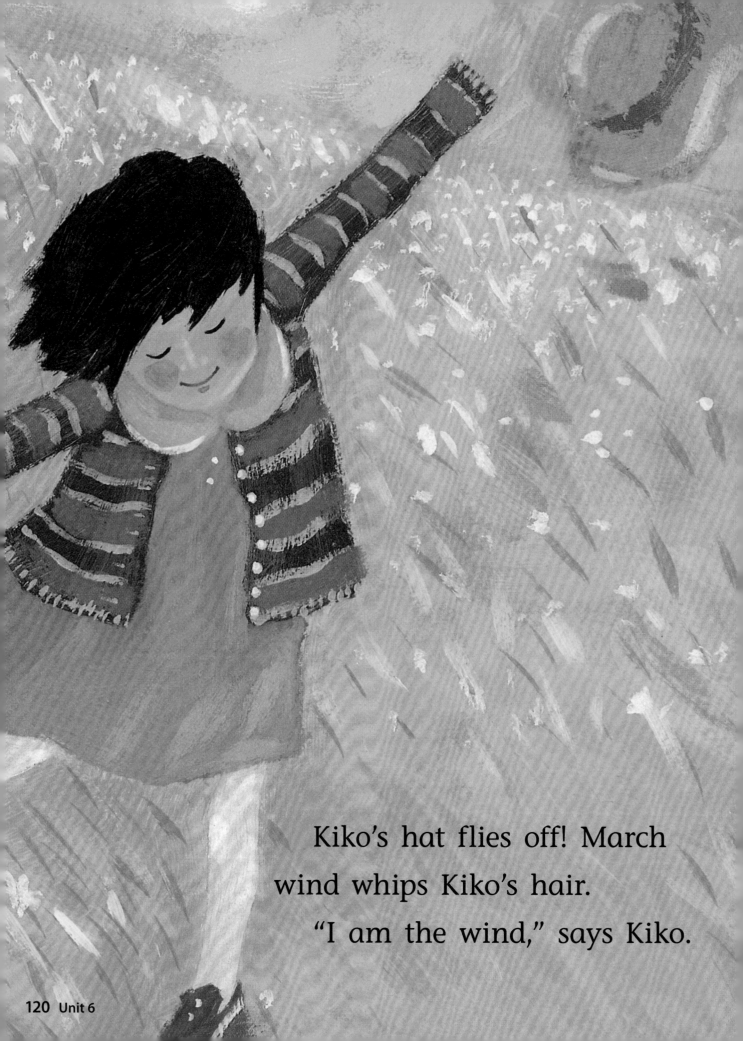

Kiko's hat flies off! March
wind whips Kiko's hair.
"I am the wind," says Kiko.

April rain falls everywhere. It waters the earth and Kiko, too. Now she must play inside.

Kiko plants a seed. Maybe it will grow big. May is a **month** for growing.

Kiko picks June strawberries. One fat berry for the basket. Many fat berries for Kiko. Inside they become Kikoberries.

July fireflies glow in the night. They blink their lights at Kiko. Kiko chases them and laughs. Her eyes are shining, too.

August mornings are **hot**. Kiko wears her bathing suit. She sits in her pool. Now August feels **cool**.

Crickets chirp at Kiko. Together they sing a September song.

Red and gold leaves are falling. Kiko holds a red leaf in one hand. She holds a gold leaf in the other. Kiko feels like an October tree.

Kiko looks for the moon. The orange moon is hiding. When Kiko hides, the moon finds her. Kiko and the November moon are playing.

In December Kiko breathes out
clouds. She puts on her winter coat.
She wears her mittens and hat.
Kiko is ready for snow. ❖

## Meet the Author

# Ferida Wolff

Ferida Wolff wrote a lot when she was a young girl. She wrote about people and pets. She wrote letters and stories.

Ms. Wolff still writes many stories. There is always something new to learn and write about.

▲ Ferida Wolff

### Writing Tip 🖉

Find words that Ferida Wolff used to tell what Kiko does. Can you think of other action words?

## Talk About It

**1.** What does Kiko do in the **month** of May?

Kiko _____ in the month of May.

**2.** Why does Kiko wear a hat and gloves when she plays in the snow?

She wears them because _____ .

**3.** Does Kiko like July? How do you know?

Kiko _____ July. She _____ .

## Write About It

Find one sensory detail in "A Year for Kiko."
Fill in these sentences.

The sensory detail word is _____ .
This tells me Kiko _____ .

# Classify Details

What does Kiko do in different weather?

**Classification Chart**

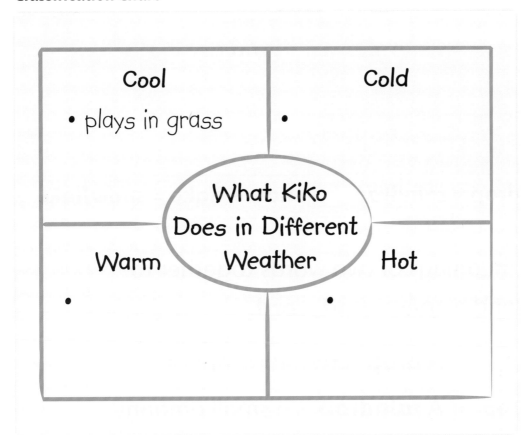

| Cool | Cold |
|---|---|
| • plays in grass | • |

*What Kiko Does in Different Weather*

| Warm | Hot |
|---|---|
| • | • |

Use your chart and the illustrations in the story to retell what Kiko does in different weather.

# Compound Words

| raindrop | snowflake |
|---|---|
| rain + drop = raindrop | snow + flake = snowflake |

Put the meanings of two words together to understand a **compound word**.

**drop**
- A **drop** is a small amount.

**rain + drop**
- A **raindrop** is a small amount of rain.

## Try It Together

Put these words together to make compound words. Use what you know about each word to tell what it means.

| fire | + | flies | = | fireflies |
|---|---|---|---|---|
| Kiko | + | berries | = | Kikoberries |
| moon | + | light | = | moonlight |

**Making Connections** Learn more about how weather can be wild.

**Genre** In an **interview**, one person asks questions while another person answers them.

# Chasing Storms
## with Tim Samaras

by **Jennifer Tetzloff**

Most people run from tornadoes. Not Tim Samaras. He was a storm chaser.

# What is a storm chaser?

A storm chaser follows thunderstorms that create tornadoes to learn more about them.

# What is a tornado?

**thunderstorm**

**tornado**

A tornado starts as a powerful thunderstorm. The storm creates spinning, funnel-shaped clouds. If the clouds touch the ground, then it is a tornado.

## Where and when do tornadoes happen?

Tornadoes can happen anywhere. Most tornadoes happen between March and August.

## Why do storm chasers study tornadoes?

Tornadoes are dangerous. Learning about tornadoes helps keep people safe. ❖

# Compare Genres

How are the words in "A Year for Kiko" and "Chasing Storms with Tim Samaras" different?

**Realistic Fiction**

July fireflies glow in the night. They blink their lights at Kiko. Kiko chases them and laughs. Her eyes are shining, too.

124 Unit 6

has sensory details and characters

**Interview**

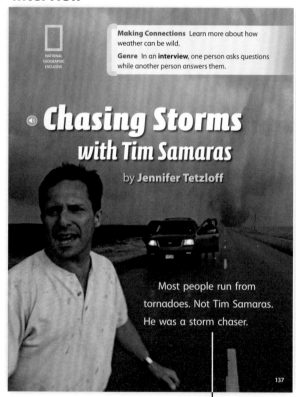

Making Connections Learn more about how weather can be wild.

Genre In an interview, one person asks questions while another person answers them.

# Chasing Storms
## with Tim Samaras
by Jennifer Tetzloff

Most people run from tornadoes. Not Tim Samaras. He was a storm chaser.

137

has facts about real people

**Talk Together**

Think about what you read. What's wild about weather?

# Ask Questions

Ask a **question** to get **information**.

## Grammar Rules  Ask Questions

| Questions | Information |
|---|---|
| Who is that? | That is Tim.  |
| What is that? | It is a tornado. |
| Where is the tornado? | It is far away. |
| Why is it so windy? | It is windy because of the tornado. |
| When did it start raining? | It started at 4:00. |
| How is the weather? | It is rainy. |

## Read a Sentence

What information do these questions ask about?
How do you know?

1. Who was a storm chaser?
2. How does a tornado start?

## Write a Sentence

Write a question for a storm chaser. Ask for information about this job.

# Write Like a Reporter

## Write a Nonfiction Paragraph

What do you know about weather? Explain what happens on a windy, rainy, sunny, or snowy day. Write a paragraph for your classmates.

### A Rainy Day

**A paragraph has an indent.**

Kids wear raincoats. They jump in puddles. You hear thunder. Boom! This all happens because the weather is rainy. Rain falls from the sky.

A nonfiction paragraph tells about something real that happens.

It also tells why things happen.

- ____ happens because the weather is ____ .

## ❶ Plan and Write

Talk about kinds of weather with a partner. Pick one kind of weather. Explain to your partner what happens because of this weather.

Write a sentence that tells about the kind of weather. Then write sentences to explain what happens because of this weather.

## ❷ Check Your Work

Revise and edit your writing. Use this checklist.

## ❸ Finish and Share

Finish your paragraph. Write each sentence neatly. Leave space between each word.

Read your paragraph clearly. Listen politely when other reporters read.

### Checklist

☑ Did you use any compound words? Can you add one?

☑ Check your sentences. Did you use the right end marks?

☑ Read each word of your paragraph. Check the spelling. Look for missing letters. Correct spelling errors.

Sometimes we hear thunder on a rainy day.

# Share Your Ideas

Think about the different kinds of weather.
What's wild about weather? Choose one of
these ways to share your ideas about the
**Big Question**.

## Write It! ✏️

**Draw and Write**
Draw a picture of
a storm. Write two
sentences about the
storm. Tell how it
looks and sounds.

The sky is dark. The thunder is loud.

## Talk About It!

### Weather Report

Pretend that you are a weather person on TV. Give your weather report to the group. Describe the weather today. Tell what the weather will be like tomorrow.

> Today it is sunny and warm.

## Do It!

### Make Air Move

Work with a partner. Make a fan, kite, or other type of air mover. Explain to your partner how your invention works.

# Then and Now

What's the difference between then and now?

CHONGQING, CHINA
Reinventing vintage photographs on smartphones

**Unit at a Glance**
- **Language Focus**: Express Opinions, Express Feelings
- **Reading Strategy**: Visualize
- **Phonics Focus**: Digraphs: *th, sh*; Vowel Sounds and Spellings: *er, ir, ur*
- **Topic**: Then and Now

## Share What You Know

**Do It!**

❶ **Act out** something you do with a machine. Let the class guess.

❷ **Discuss** what people did before they had that machine.

## Express Opinions

Listen and sing.

**Words to Know**

do

not

think

**Song**

# Call Me

I think it would be great
To hear your voice.
I think it would be great
To hear your voice.

You could write a letter.
But I think
The phone is better.

I do not think a letter
Is a good choice.

Tune: "If You're Happy and You Know It"

## 🔊 Key Words

How do people talk and share **news**?

| Then | Now |
|------|-----|
| write a letter | write an e-mail (computer) |
| read a newspaper | read news on the **Internet** |
| talk on the phone | send a text **message** |

**Talk Together**

Look at the ways we communicate. What's the difference between then and now? What do you think is the best way to communicate?

# Identify Main Idea and Details

**Main Idea and Details Diagram**

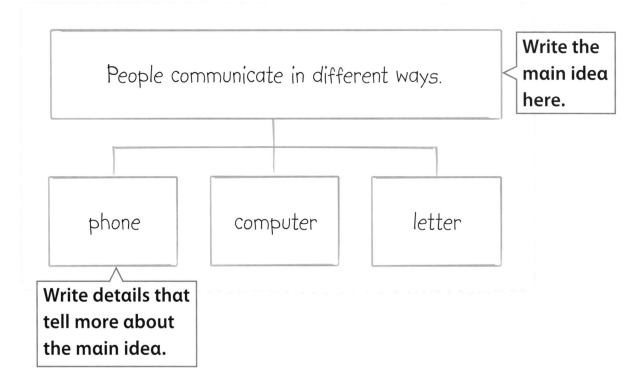

People communicate in different ways.

Write the main idea here.

phone    computer    letter

Write details that tell more about the main idea.

Look for the main idea and details as you listen and read.

**Talk Together**

Use gestures to show how you communicate. Your partner guesses what you are doing. Take turns. Then add ways you communicate to the chart.

## ◀)) More Key Words

**past** **present** **future**

In the **past**, I was in kindergarten.

Today is the **present**. I am in first grade.

In the **future**, I will be in second grade.

**communicate**

People **communicate** by talking and writing.

**history**

Study **history** to learn what happened long ago.

**Talk Together**

Make **Key Word** cards. Pick one, and use the word in a sentence.

> I learn about the present by watching today's news on TV.

# Digraphs: *sh, th*

shell

feather

**Listen** and **Learn**

Listen to the picture words. Choose the correct letters to complete each word.

**1.**

__ __ e m

**2.**

__ __ i p

**3.**

m o __ __ e r

**4.**

f i __ __

Listen and read. Find the words with the digraphs *sh* or *th*.

## A Different Time

The class was learning about history.

"There were no computers in the past," said their teacher.

"I'm shocked!" said Shane. "I do not think that can be true."

"It is," replied the teacher. "People didn't have the Internet. They read books."

"How did they send email messages?" asked Sasha.

"They didn't," said the teacher. "They sent letters. They got their news from newspapers."

"At least they didn't have to worry about computers breaking down," laughed Chico.

> **Work with a partner.**
> Take turns. Point to a word with *sh* or *th*. Your partner says the word and then spells it.

◄ Practice reading words with *sh* and *th* by reading "A Different Time" with a partner.

# Read a History Article

A **history article** is nonfiction. It describes what life was like in the past.

## Timeline

A timeline shows when things happened.

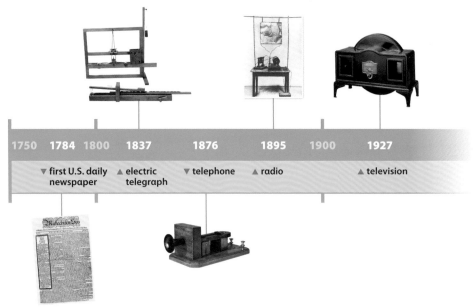

| 1750 | 1784 | 1800 | 1837 | 1876 | 1895 | 1900 | 1927 |
|------|------|------|------|------|------|------|------|

▼ first U.S. daily newspaper   ▲ electric telegraph   ▼ telephone   ▲ radio   ▲ television

▲ This timeline shows years.

## Reading Strategy

As you read, use the words and pictures to **visualize** what things were like in the past.

# ◀)) **Communication**
## Then and Now

### by **Robin Nelson**

**Communication is sharing ideas and news.**
**Most people communicate by talking and writing.**
**People can use their bodies to communicate, too.**

**Communication has changed. <mark>Now</mark>, people <mark>communicate</mark> better and faster.**

Long ago, people made pictures to tell stories. The pictures could be drawings or symbols.

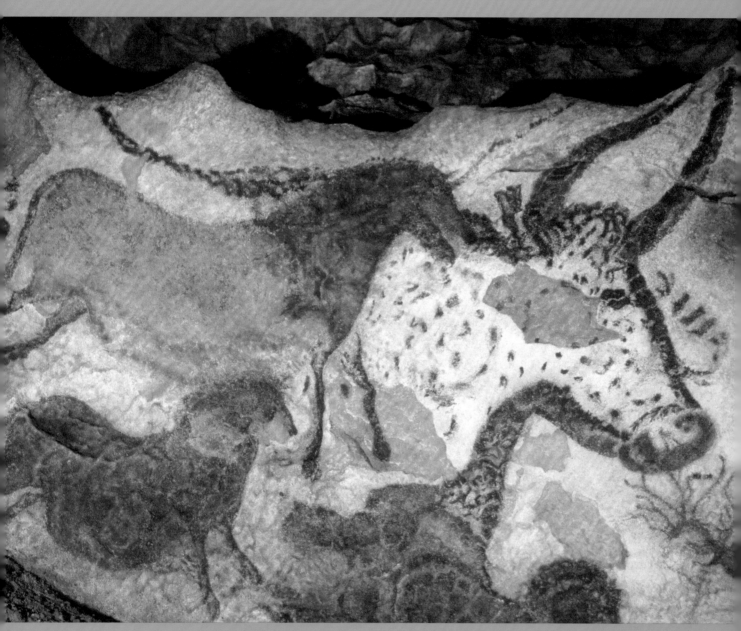

▲ This painting was discovered in a cave in France.

…S IN A HOUSE.

A SISTER

A D

**Now**, people use words more often to tell stories.

Long ago, people copied each book.
If they wanted 10 copies of a book, they
had to write out each copy one at a time.

▲ This book was written with a feather
pen and bottles of ink in 1453.

feather pen

ink

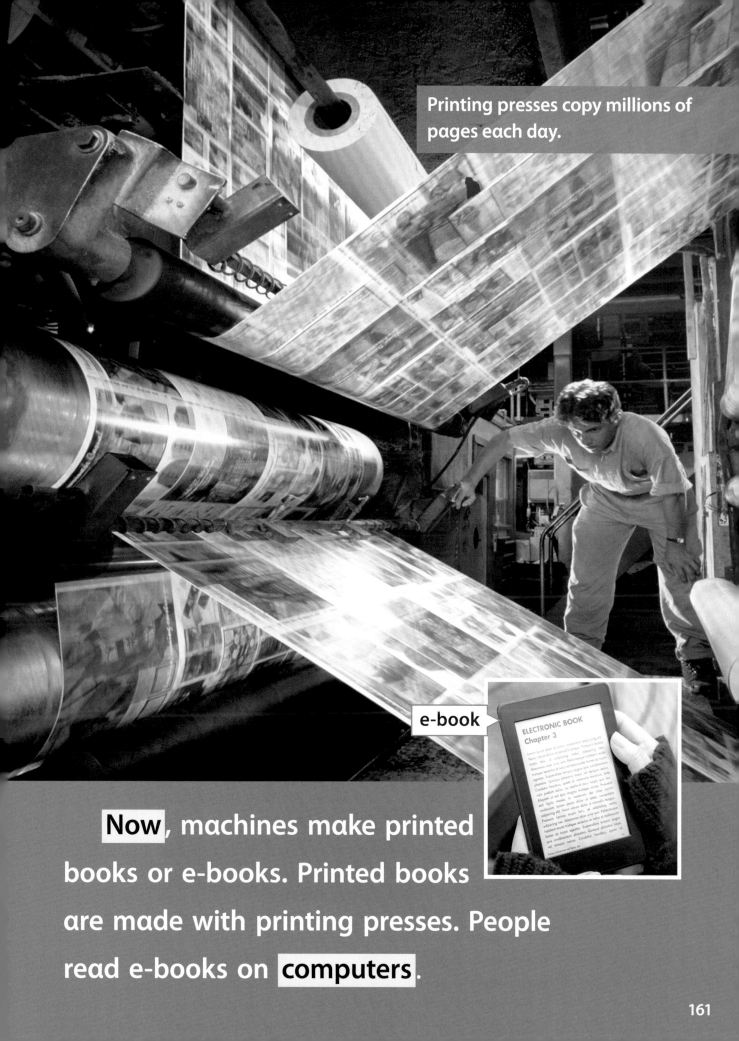

Printing presses copy millions of pages each day.

e-book

ELECTRONIC BOOK
Chapter 3

Now, machines make printed books or e-books. Printed books are made with printing presses. People read e-books on computers.

161

Long ago, people tapped **messages** on telegraph machines. Telegraph machines sent messages using electricity. It took about a minute to send each word.

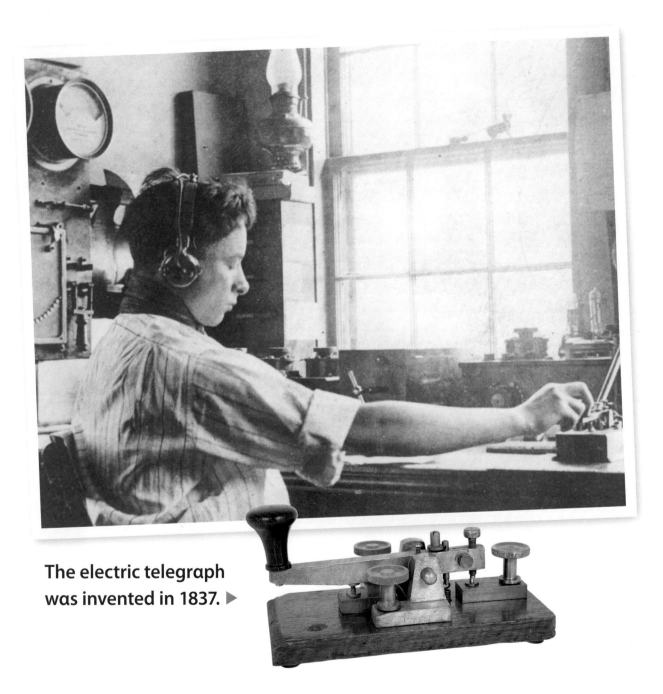

The electric telegraph was invented in 1837. ▶

The telephone was invented in 1876 by Alexander Graham Bell.

cell phone

cord

**Now**, people call each other on telephones. Most people have cell phones. Long ago, telephones always needed cords.

Long ago, people wrote letters. It could take months to mail a letter. Mail went on ships and by horses. Today, mail delivery is done by trucks and planes so letters are delivered much quicker.

▲ People wrote letters using pens and paper.

ink

ink pen

**Now**, people write e-mails on **computers**. An e-mail **message** can be delivered in just seconds. Today, many people write e-mail messages instead of hand-written letters.

e-mail message

| Mail | File | Edit | View | Mailbox | Messa |

| Send | Chat | Attach | Fonts | Colors | Save As Draft | Bigger | Print |

To: Anna
Cc:
Subject: Morning!

Hi there,

Thanks for the e-mail - good to hear it's going well.

165

Newspapers were sold on street corners. This newspaper was sold in New York in 1881. ▶

Long ago, hundreds of people read newspapers. The first United States daily newspaper was published in 1784. People had to buy a newspaper to read it.

Many people get newspapers delivered to them at home.

**Now**, millions of people read newspapers. People can buy printed newspapers.

People can also read newspapers on the **Internet**. People all over the world can read **news** on the Internet.

Internet news

laptop computer

Long ago, people could only listen to **news** on radios. Radios only make sounds. They do not have pictures.

▲ The radio was invented in 1895.

**Now**, people can watch **news** on televisions.

Communication will continue to change. What do you think will happen next? ❖

The TV was invented in 1927.

# Communication Timeline

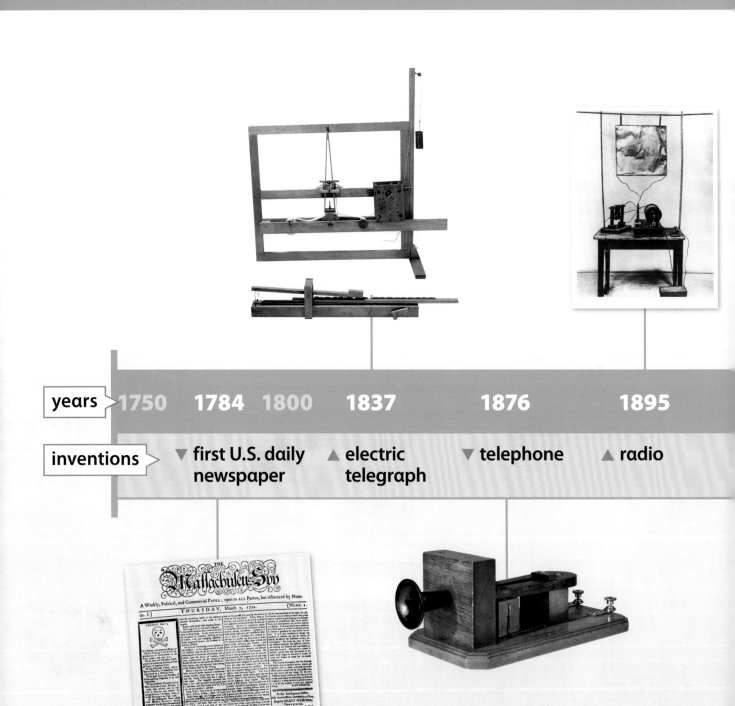

| years | 1750 | 1784 | 1800 | 1837 | 1876 | 1895 |
|-------|------|------|------|------|------|------|

| inventions | ▼ first U.S. daily newspaper | ▲ electric telegraph | ▼ telephone | ▲ radio |
|------------|------|------|------|------|

| 1900 | 1927 | 1943 | 1972 | 1985 | 2000 |

▲ television  ▼ computer  ▲ e-mail  ▼ first cell phones used

171

# Talk About It

**1.** How do people **communicate**?

People communicate by ____ and ____ .

**2.** How is communication different **now** than it was in the **past**? Look back in the text and name two details.

Now, people ____ . Then, people ____ .

**3.** Why is the **computer** an important invention?

People can ____ and ____ on a computer.

# Write About It

What is your favorite way to communicate? Why?

I like to ____ because ____ .

# Identify Main Idea and Details

Add details to show how communication has changed.

**Main Idea and Details Diagram**

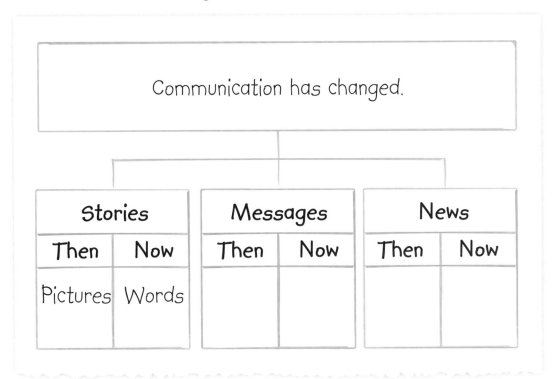

| Communication has changed. | | | | | |
|---|---|---|---|---|---|

| Stories | | Messages | | News | |
|---|---|---|---|---|---|
| Then | Now | Then | Now | Then | Now |
| Pictures | Words | | | | |

Use your chart to tell how communication has changed.

"Long ago, people drew stories with pictures."

"Now, people write stories with words."

# Alphabetize and Use a Dictionary

| Words in Alphabetical Order |
| --- |
| computer |
| e-mail |
| Internet |
| radio |

Words in **alphabetical order** are listed by their first letters. They go in the order of the alphabet.

**Try It Together**

With a partner, put these words in alphabetical order. Use a dictionary to find each word's meaning.

| |
| --- |
| telephone |
| newspaper |
| book |
| machine |

**Making Connections** You read about **communication** **now** and in the **past**. Now read about inventions for the **future**.

**Genre** A **blog** is an **Internet** journal. This **blog entry** is nonfiction. It gives information about space inventions.

Space Adventures

https://eltngl.com/reachhigherseries

# Space Adventures

MAIN SCREEN | PICTURES | LINKS | SIGN IN

Date: August 21

## Building for Space

Scientists and engineers design things to help astronauts explore outer space. They need to figure out how human beings can live, breathe, and work in space.

Search

LINKS

▸ Space News

▸ Astronaut News

▲ A model of the International Space Station.

175

Search

LINKS

▸ Space News

▸ Astronaut News

Space is not like earth. The air is different. Astronauts have to wear special clothing. They bring air to breathe. They float around in space. It is fun to watch!

helmet

air to breathe

astronaut

▶ Read More About Astronauts

Scientists are building spaceships that astronauts will fly to the moon and nearby planets. In the **future**, there might even be buildings on the moon!

moon

Next »

Search

LINKS

▸ Space News

▸ Astronaut News

Spaceships use cameras and **computers** to **communicate**. The computers can send **messages** and pictures back to Earth.

The first spaceship that flew to the moon did not have enough power for a long visit. **Now**, we can make more powerful spaceships.

**Then**: The Apollo 11 spaceship in 1969.

Who knows where we will go next? It is fun to imagine where we will be able to go in the **future**! ❖

**Now:** This is the design for a new spacecraft called Orion.

**Posted by Brian**    August 24  9:00 a.m.

Older Posts »

**MAIN SCREEN** | PICTURES | LINKS                                | SIGN IN

# Compare Genres

Think about "Communication Then and Now" and "Space Adventures." How are they alike and different?

**Venn Diagram**

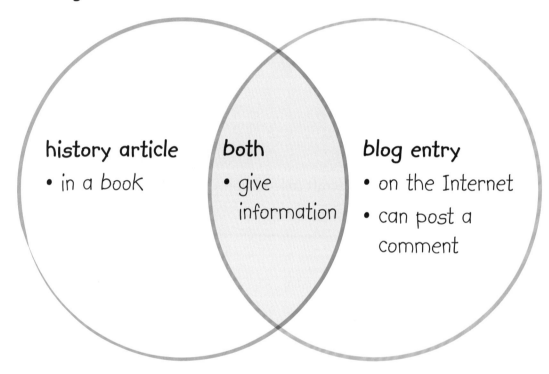

history article
• in a book

both
• give information

blog entry
• on the Internet
• can post a comment

Look through the texts. Add to the diagram.

**Talk Together**

Think about what you read and learned. What's the difference between **then** and **now**?

# Past Tense Verbs

**Verbs** can tell about actions that happened in the past.

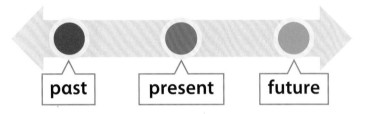

| past | present | future |

## Grammar Rules  Past Tense Verbs

| To make a verb about the past:<br><br>• Add **-ed** to the end of a **regular verb**, like **want**. | Today people **want** to build new spaceships. In the past, they **wanted** to build the first spaceship. |
| --- | --- |
| • Use a special form for an **irregular verb**, like **fly**. | Today people **fly** to space. In the past, they **flew** to space for the first time. |

## Read a Sentence

Read page 162. Find two verbs in the past tense. Explain their forms.

## Write a Sentence

Write a sentence about a time you wanted to go somewhere new. Read it to a partner.

## Express Feelings

Listen and Sing.

**Song**

# New Phone

Oh, my darling. I am Marta.
My new phone is very small.
I wish I could have my old phone.
It was always on the wall.

My new phone is very modern.
I feel really glad for this.
I wish I could use my new phone,
But I don't know where it is.

Tune: "My Darling Clementine"

## 🔊 Key Words

**Old**

**New**

The old **record** player is fun to use.

But the new way to play **music** sounds **better**. It is **easier** to carry with you.

**Talk Together**

How would you feel about listening to music on a record player? Are new ways always better?

# Describe Characters' Feelings

**Character Description Chart**

| Character | What the Character Says or Does | What this Shows About How the Character Feels |
|---|---|---|
| Marta | • I wish I could have my old phone. <br><br> • I feel very glad for this. | • unhappy <br><br><br> • happy |

| Write the name of the character here. | Write what the character says or does here. | Write how the character feels here. |
|---|---|---|

I feel sad that I don't have those shoes anymore.

**Talk Together**

What do you wish you could have from the past? Describe your feelings about it to a partner.

# 🔊 More Key Words

## build

You can **build** things with blocks.

## invent

People **invent** things like the telephone.

## machine

This **machine** washes dishes.

## modern

This cell phone is more **modern** than the old phone.

## tool

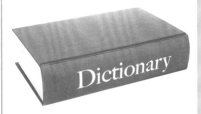

A dictionary is a **tool** you can use to look up words.

### Talk Together

Draw a picture of a **Key Word** for a partner to label.

tool

# 🔊 Vowel Sounds and Spellings: *er, ir, ur*

fern

girl

nurse

**Listen** and **Learn**

🔊 Listen to each group of words. Choose the two words in each group with the vowel sound you hear in the word *her*.

1. turn     ton     bird
2. better   dirt    dot
3. nurse    nose    purse
4. stir     turn    tune
5. burn     bun     burst
6. form     firm    fur

🔊 Listen and read. Find the words with the vowel sound you hear in the word *her.*

## Modern Machines

Tyler pointed to a picture of a modern machine. "I am glad I don't live in the past," he said. "I feel we are lucky. Machines make our lives easier."

"I would like to be the first girl to invent a new tool. It would clean up the oceans," said Amber. "What would you invent?"

"A time machine," said Tyler. "I want to turn back the clock just a little bit. Then I could take my math test over. I would get a perfect score!"

**Work with a partner.**
Take turns. Choose a word with the vowel sound you hear in the word *her.* Use the word in a sentence.

◄ Read "Modern Machines" with a partner. Practice reading words with the vowel sound you hear in the word *her.*

# Read a Story

**Realistic fiction** has events that are not real but could happen in real life.

## Characters' Feelings

Look for words that tell you how characters feel. Then think about why the characters have these feelings.

feeling word

"I love music just like you do."

## Reading Strategy

As you read, use the words and pictures to **visualize** how the characters feel and why.

# A New Old Tune

by **Pat Cummings**

illustrated by

**Frank Morrison**

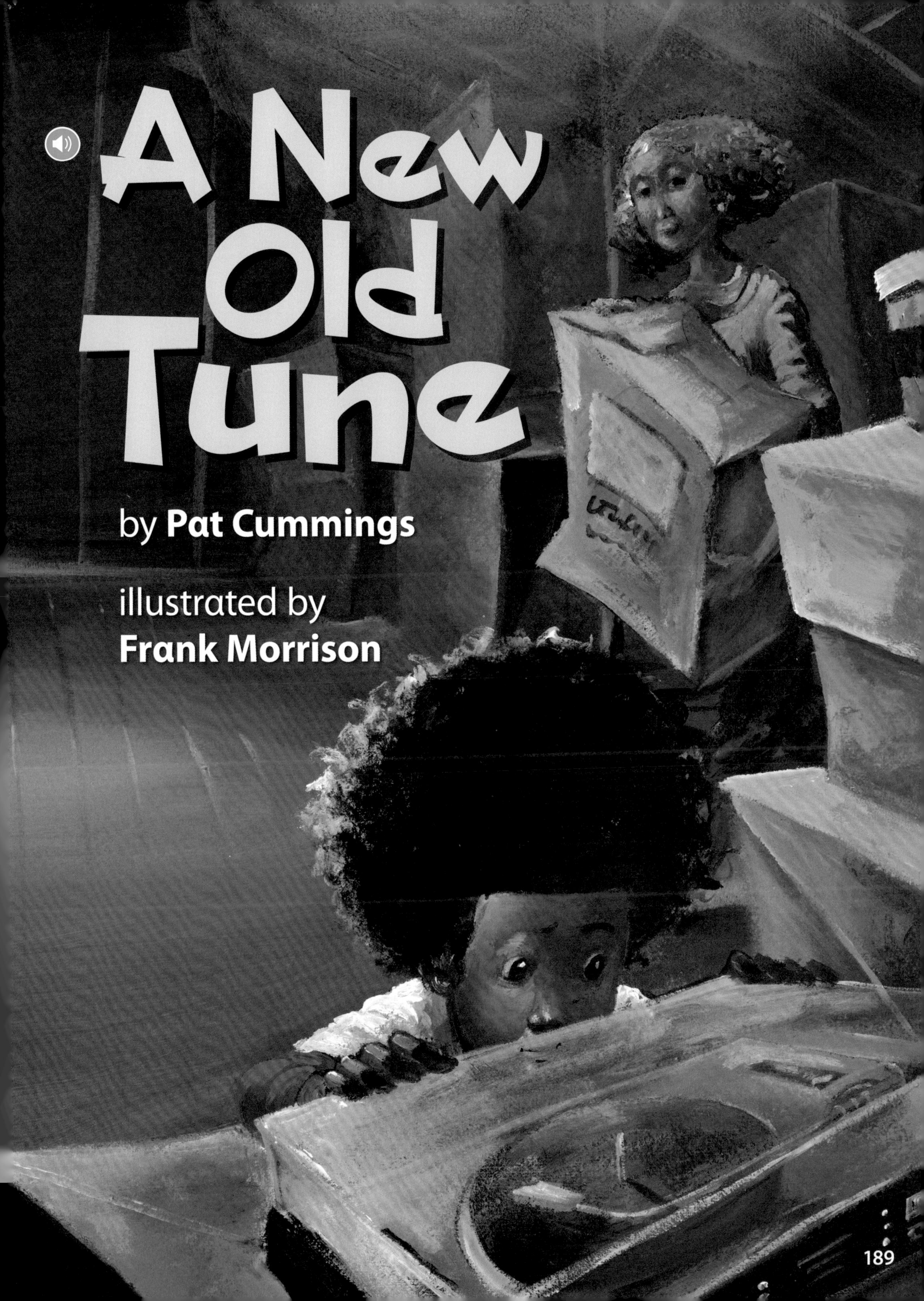

"What is this, Aunt Nell?" asked Max. He was helping his aunt choose things to sell at her yard sale.

"This disk must go into a giant computer!" Max said. Aunt Nell shook her head.

"That is a **record**," Aunt Nell said.
"I love **music** just like you do."

Aunt Nell pulled out a stack of black disks.

"Wow," said Max. "How do they work?"

Aunt Nell opened a dusty, wooden box. She plugged it into the wall. "This is my old record player."

Music filled the attic.

"But you can't carry it with you!" Max said.

"No one carried **music** players back then,"
Aunt Nell said. "I played music on this
**record** player at home. My friends would
listen, too. Then we would dance together."

"Things change," Aunt Nell said. "Television used to be just black and white."

"You had TV way back then?" Max asked.

"Hey, I'm not that **old**!" Aunt Nell said.

Max and Aunt Nell got back
to work. There was an **old** camera
she wanted to sell. There were
photo albums she wanted to keep.

Max saw a picture of a young Aunt Nell talking on a phone. It had a long, curly cord.

"Did you like those **old** phones **better**?" Max asked.

"No," Aunt Nell smiled. "Some **new** things are much **easier** to use."

"But some **old** things are pretty neat," Max said. He looked at the **record** player. "Will you dance with me?" Max asked.

"Yes," said Aunt Nell. She turned up the **music**.

"Has anything stayed the same?" asked Max.

"Yes," said Aunt Nell. "People still love to talk on the telephone. And watch television. And listen to **music**."

"And dance!" added Max.

"Maybe I'll keep these old records," Aunt Nell sighed.

"Or you could burn them onto a music player," Max said.

"BURN them?" Aunt Nell gasped.

Max groaned. It was his turn to explain. ❖

# Pat Cummings

AWARD WINNER

**Pat Cummings** moved often when she was young. Her father was in the army. She used to draw pictures all the time. She joined art clubs to meet new friends.

Ms. Cummings writes about things she knows. She is always thinking about her next story!

Pat Cummings ▶

## Writing Tip

Pat Cummings helps readers learn about her characters' feelings by using verbs. Can you find examples of this in the story?

# Talk About It

**1.** What was Max helping Aunt Nell do?

Max was helping Aunt Nell ____ .

**2.** How are Max and Aunt Nell the same?
What do they both like?

Max and Aunt Nell both like ____ .

**3.** Think about your own photos. Why does
Aunt Nell want to keep her photo albums?

Aunt Nell wants to keep them because ____ .

# Write About It

What does your family own that is **old** ?
What do you think about it?

We have an old ____ . I think it is ____ .

# Describe Characters' Feelings

What do Max and Nell say or do? What does this show about how they feel?

**Character Description Chart**

| Character | What the Character Says or Does | What This Shows About How the Character Feels |
|---|---|---|
| Max | • Wow<br><br>• | • He feels surprised.<br><br>• |
| Nell | •<br><br>• | •<br><br>• |

Use your chart to talk about Max and Nell. Why do they feel like they do?

# Alphabetize and Use a Dictionary

## Words in Alphabetical Order

**ma**chine

**me**ssage

**mo**dern

These words are in **alphabetical order**. Each word begins with the same letter. The second letter of each word is used to put them in order.

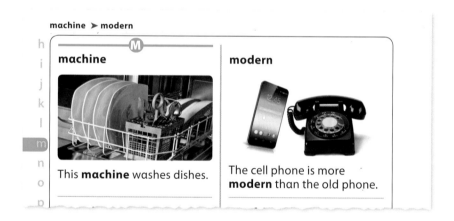

machine ➤ modern

**machine**

This **machine** washes dishes.

**modern**

The cell phone is more **modern** than the old phone.

### Try It Together

With a partner, write these words on cards. Put the words in alphabetical order. Use a dictionary to find the word's meaning. Then read your list aloud.

| cell phone |
| camera |
| cord |

**Making Connections** You read about **old** and **new** ways to play **music**. Now read about old inventions that are still used today.

**Genre** A **poem** uses rhyme and rhythm to describe something in a special way.

# Invention Poems

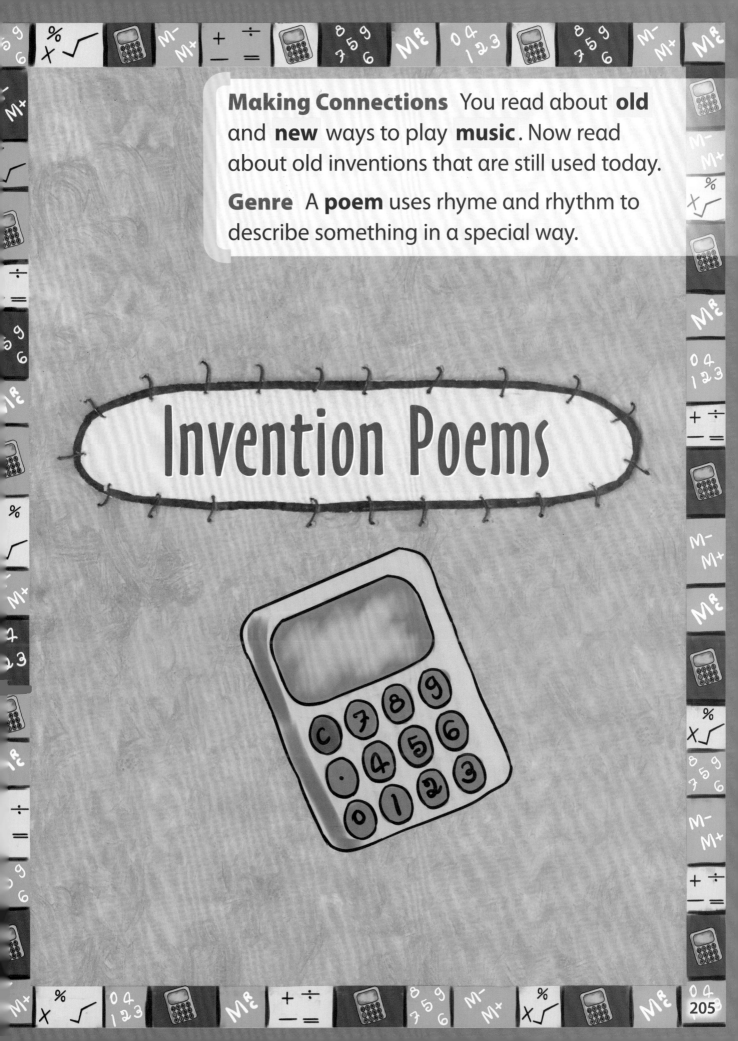

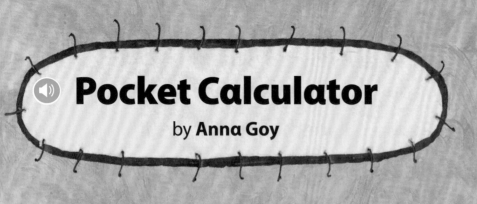

# Pocket Calculator

by **Anna Goy**

Curt was always the best in his class,
And the subject he was most interested
in was Math.
He tried adding with his fingers and toes.
But for big numbers
he wrote too many zeroes.

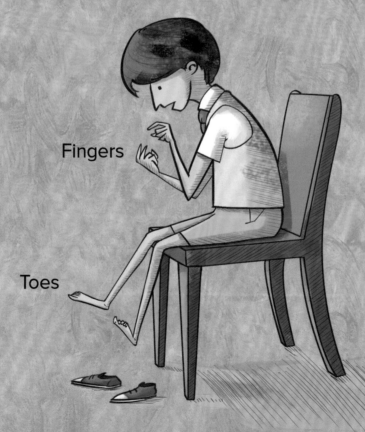

Fingers

Toes

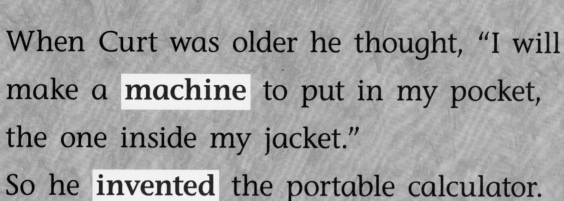

When Curt was older he thought, "I will make a **machine** to put in my pocket, the one inside my jacket."

So he **invented** the portable calculator.

And as if by magic his life was **easier**. ❖

Curt Herzstark was from Austria. He invented the Curta Calculator in the 1930s. It was the first calculator that could fit in one hand—or a pocket!

# Past and Present

by **Hector Sanchez**

When I think about
The present and the past,
I think about **machines**
That move slow and fast.

Clunky cars used to creep
So super slow,
Now they zip and zoom
And go, go, go! ❖

# Compare Genres

"A New Old Tune" is realistic fiction. "Pocket Calculator" and "Past and Present" are poems. Find connections between these texts.

**Realistic Fiction**

"No one carried **music** players back then," Aunt Nell said. "I played music on this **record** player at home. My friends would listen, too. Then we would dance together."

194 Unit 7

**Poem**

**Pocket Calculator**
by Anna Goy

Curt was always the best in his class,
And the subject he was most interested in was Math.
He tried adding with his fingers and toes.
But for big numbers
he wrote too many zeroes.

Fingers

Toes

206 Unit 7

**They both talk about things from the past.**

**Talk Together**

Talk about what life was like before **machines**.
What is the difference between then and now?

# Future Tense Verbs

Some **verbs** tell about actions that will happen in the future.

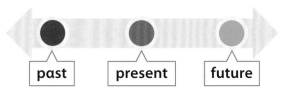

past | present | future

---

## Grammar Rules  Future Tense Verbs

| **To make verbs about the future:** | |
| --- | --- |
| • Add **will** before the verb. | • He **will** invent. |
| Add these verbs after the subject and before the main verb:<br>• I **am going to**<br>• He/She/It **is going to**<br>• They **are going to** | • He **is going to** make a machine. |

---

## Read a Sentence

Does this sentence tell about the future? Explain.

I will make a machine to put in my pocket.

## Write a Sentence

Write a sentence about what machines will do in the future. Read it to a partner.

# Write as a Friend

## Write a Friendly Letter

What do you know about things from the past? Describe something old you have seen. Write a letter to a friend.

Write your friend's name in the **greeting**.

In the **body** of the letter, tell your news. This could include a **main idea** and details.

Write a **closing** and sign your name.

October 1

Dear Manny,

Last week, my dad showed me an old phone. The old phone did not have buttons. It had a dial with numbers. It had holes for your fingers.

The next day, I took the phone to school. We all dialed our phone numbers! I think old things are fun to use.

Your friend,

Aliya

**1 Plan and Write**

Talk about things from the past with a partner. Draw a picture of one old thing. Write a list of details. Discuss your main idea. Tell your partner what you think about old things.

Write the main idea. Then write sentences with details. Remember to express your opinion.

**2 Check Your Work**

Revise and edit your writing. Use this checklist.

**3 Finish and Share**

Finish your letter. Make sure the greeting and other features of a letter are correct.

Read your letter to a friend. Share your opinions.

**Checklist**

☑ Think about different words you can use. Can you use compound words, synonyms, or antonyms?

☑ Did you use past tense and future tense verbs correctly?

☑ Trade work with a partner. Check for words that sound alike. Does the word meaning make sense in the sentence?

I think old things are too slow.

# Share Your Ideas

Think about how we do things now and how we did things in the past. What's the difference between then and now? Choose one of these ways to share your ideas about the **Big Question**.

## Write It!

### Alphabetize a List

Write a list of all the **Key Words** from the unit. Then write the words again in alphabetical order. Alphabetize to the first or second letter. Use 3 of the words to write about things you learned about the past.

# Talk About It!

### Interview a Time Traveler

Pretend you are a time traveler. You are from the past. What is life like? What do you do? Have the group ask you questions. Then have another student pretend to be from the future. Ask more questions.

I am from the past. I walk to school. We don't have a bus.

# Do It!

### Make a Telephone

Have your teacher make a hole in the bottoms of two cans. Put one piece of string through both holes. Tie knots inside the cans to hold the string. Pull the cans apart until the string is tight. One partner listens while the other partner talks.

# Get Out the Map!

? **BIG** **Question**

**Why do we need maps?**

NEWARK, NEW JERSEY, USA
Students using an interactive map in class

**Unit at a Glance**
▷ **Language Focus**: Follow Directions, Tell a Story
▷ **Reading Strategy**: Review
▷ **Phonics Focus**: Vowel Sounds and Spellings: *oi, oy; ou, ow*
▷ **Topic**: Maps

## Share What You Know

**Do It!**

❶ **Draw** your classroom.

❷ **Show** where you sit. Show the door.

❸ **Use** your drawing to give directions to a partner.

ABC

## Follow Directions

Listen and sing.

**Song**  ♪

# At the Zoo

 Oh, dear! Where
Can the monkeys be?

 Turn left. Turn right.
And you will see.

 Show me. Where
Can the monkeys be?

 This map can
Show you the way.

Tune: "Oh, Dear, What Can the Matter Be?"

You Are Here!

## 🔊 Key Words

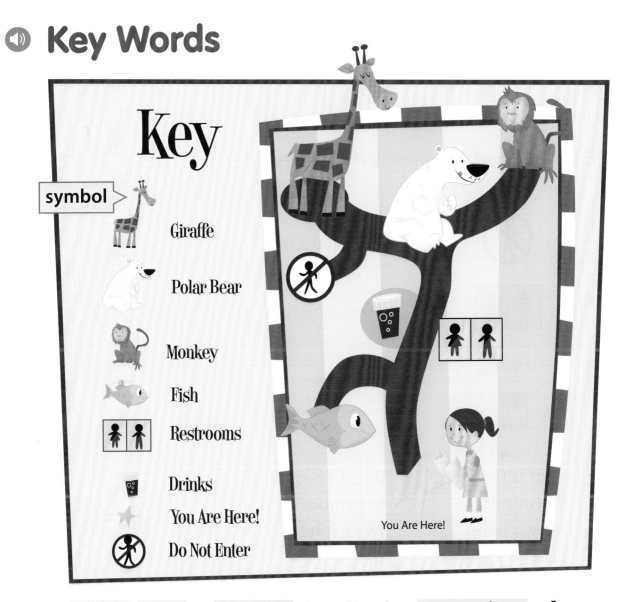

A **map key** is **useful**. It tells the **meaning** of a map's symbols. A **symbol** or sign can be a shape or a **picture**.

**Talk Together**

Tell a partner how to go from the entrance to see the fish. Use the map to help. Was the map useful?

# Use Information

**T Chart**

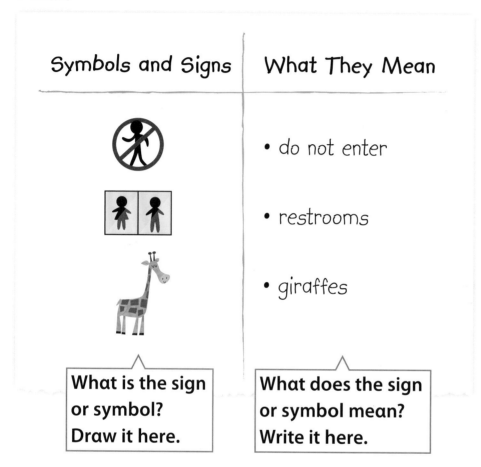

| Symbols and Signs | What They Mean |
|---|---|
| | • do not enter |
| | • restrooms |
| | • giraffes |
| **What is the sign or symbol? Draw it here.** | **What does the sign or symbol mean? Write it here.** |

**Talk Together**

Talk about the signs and **symbols** you see in your town. Draw two of them. Add them to the chart above.

# 🔊 More Key Words

## • between

The house is **between** the two trees.

## corner

Ashley Miller

I write my name in the **corner** of the paper.

## distance

This man runs a long **distance**.

## • show

I **show** my drawing.

## sign

This **sign** means "do not."

**Talk** **Together**

Use a **Key Word** to ask a question about maps.

What is the distance from your house to school?

• Words to Know

# Vowel Sounds and Spellings: *oi, oy*

coin

boy

**Listen and Learn**

Listen to each group of words. Choose the two words in each group with the vowel sound you hear in the word *boy*.

**1.** jay      joy      Joe      soy

**2.** boil      bale      ball      broil

**3.** soil      sail      toil      sell

**4.** royal      spoil      spell      spill

**5.** jail      join      just      joint

**6.** too      toy      old      oil

🔊 Listen and read. Find the words that have *oi* or *oy*.

## Lost!

"We're lost," said Roy. "Do we go right or left? I don't know which way to go."

"Let's use the map key," said Dad. "That is what a map is for. It shows where our camp is, and we can find out where we are right now. Then we will know which way to go."

"Do you mean that picture there?" Roy pointed to a picture of a tent on the map.

"Yes," his dad said. "That is a symbol for the camp. We need to turn around. We have to go that way."

"Wow, that map is not a toy. It is a useful tool," said Roy. "Now we can join the others and have lunch!"

**Work with a partner.**
Find and read each word with *oi* or *oy*. Then work together to use the words to tell what you think Roy and his dad did next.

◀ Practice reading words with the spellings *oi* or *oy* by reading "Lost!" with a partner.

# Read Informational Text

**Informational text** can explain something. This informational text explains how maps work.

## Maps

Maps use symbols. Symbols are pictures or shapes that stand for real things.

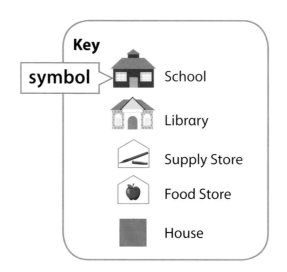

Key

symbol — School

Library

Supply Store

Food Store

House

## Reading Strategy

As you read, think of the 7 strategies you learned. Which strategies will help you understand the text?

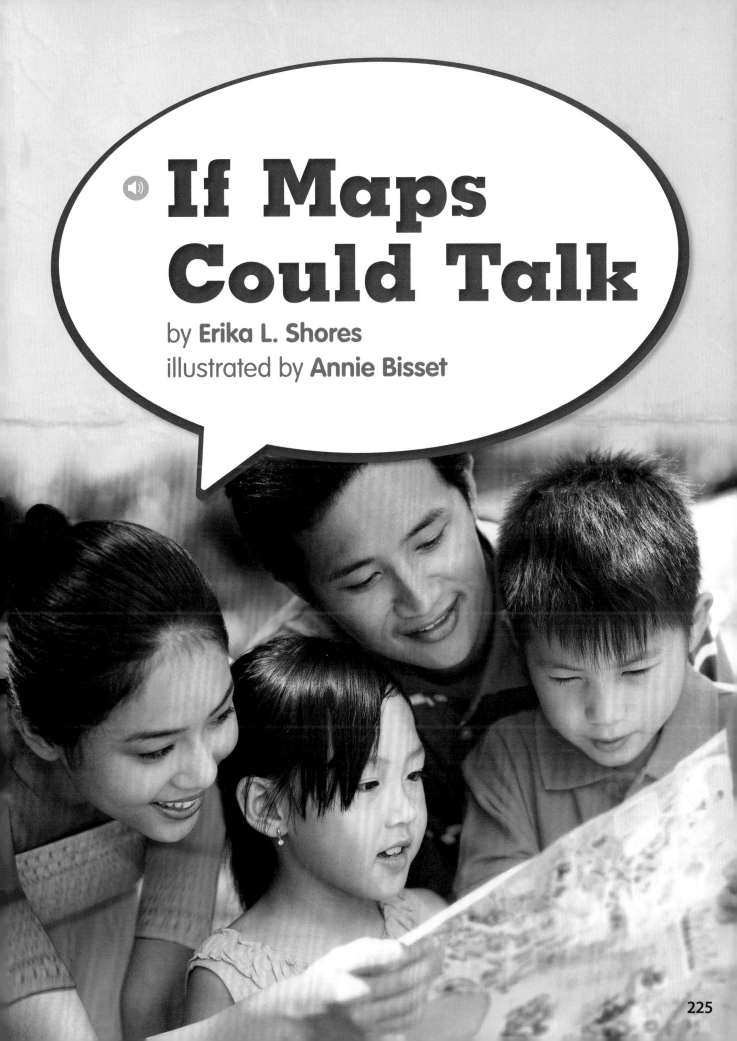

# If Maps Could Talk

by **Erika L. Shores**

illustrated by **Annie Bisset**

# Maps: Finding Your Way

Where is the water slide? If you were a bird, you could fly up high to find it. But since you are not, you will have to use a **map**.

Maps use **symbols** to **show** where things are. The orange rectangle on the **Picture** Map is a symbol for the water slide. How do you know that? Read on.

# Picture Map

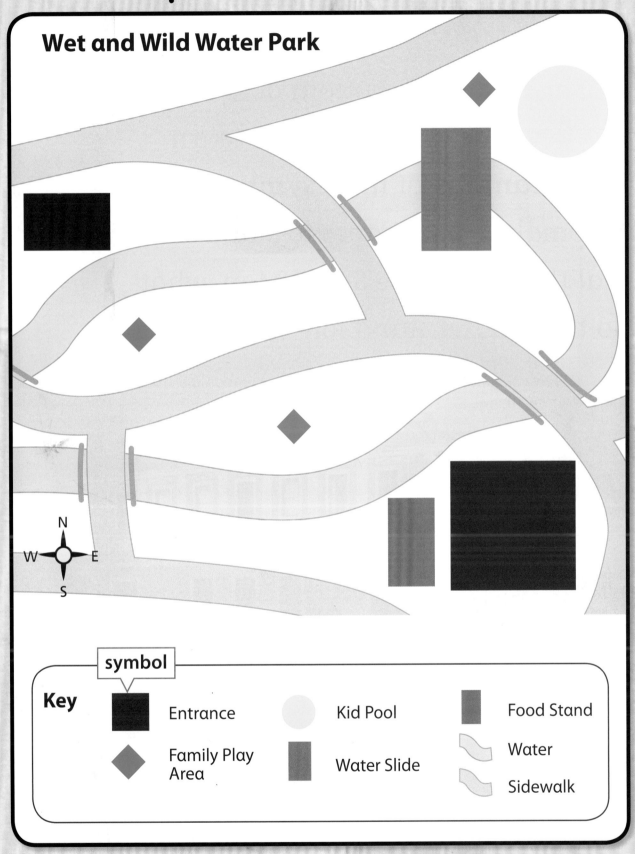

**Wet and Wild Water Park**

N
W E
S

**Key**

symbol

- ■ Entrance
- ◆ Family Play Area
- ○ Kid Pool
- ▮ Water Slide
- ▮ Food Stand
- 〰 Water
- 〰 Sidewalk

▲ A **picture map** can use shapes or **symbols** to **show** where things are.

# The Key to Using Maps

The box at the bottom of a **map** is the **key**. Use the map key to learn the **meanings** of map **symbols**. Mapmakers use shapes to stand for real things. On the Street Map, what do the squares stand for?

# Street Map

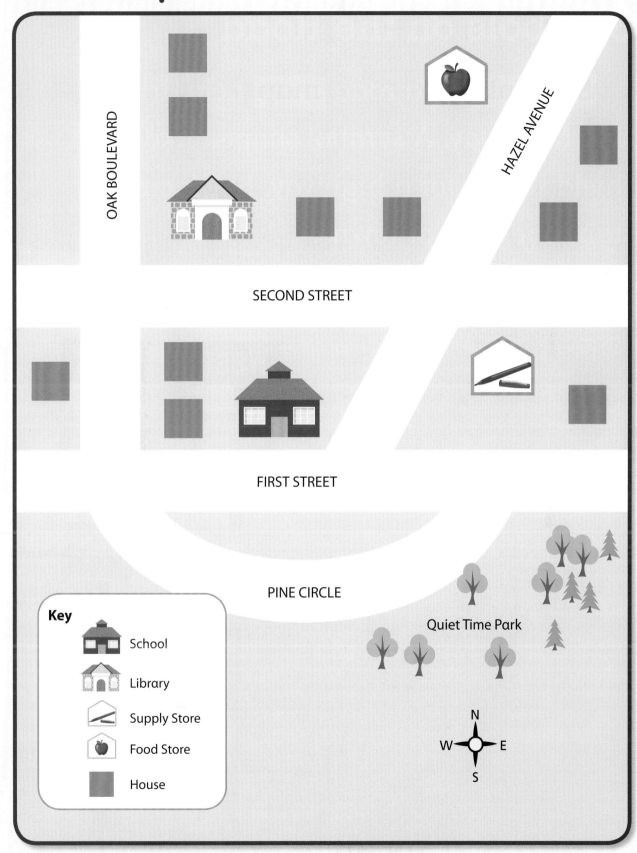

▲ A street **map shows** street names and **symbols** to help people find their way around town.

# Symbols on the Road

Symbols on a road map help drivers find their way. A symbol shaped like a shield stands for a highway. Black circles stand for cities or towns.

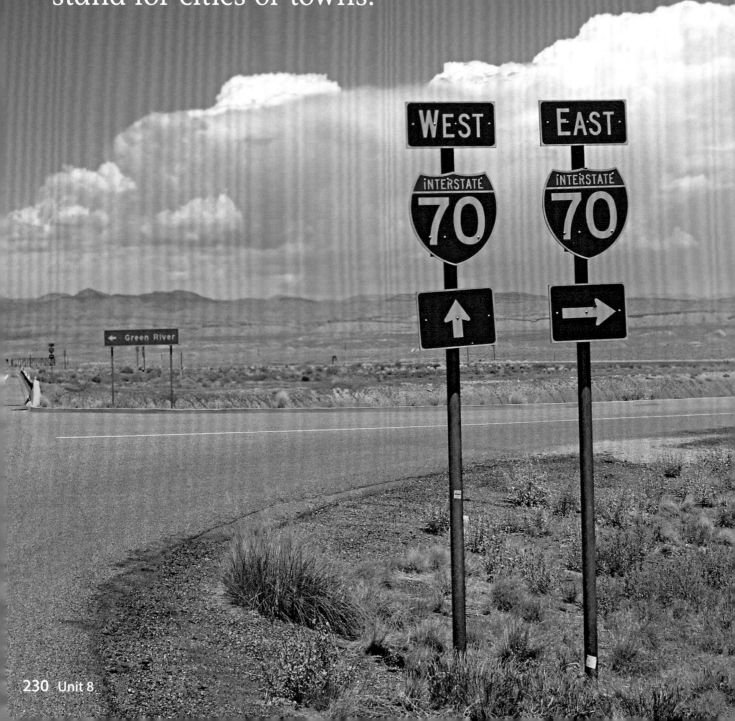

# Road Map

▲ A road **map** **shows** where roads and cities are.

# Rain or Shine:
# Weather Symbols

What will the weather be like tomorrow? Look at a weather **map** in your city's newspaper.

**Symbols** on the Weather Map **show** the weather. Use the **key** to understand what the symbols mean.

# Weather Map

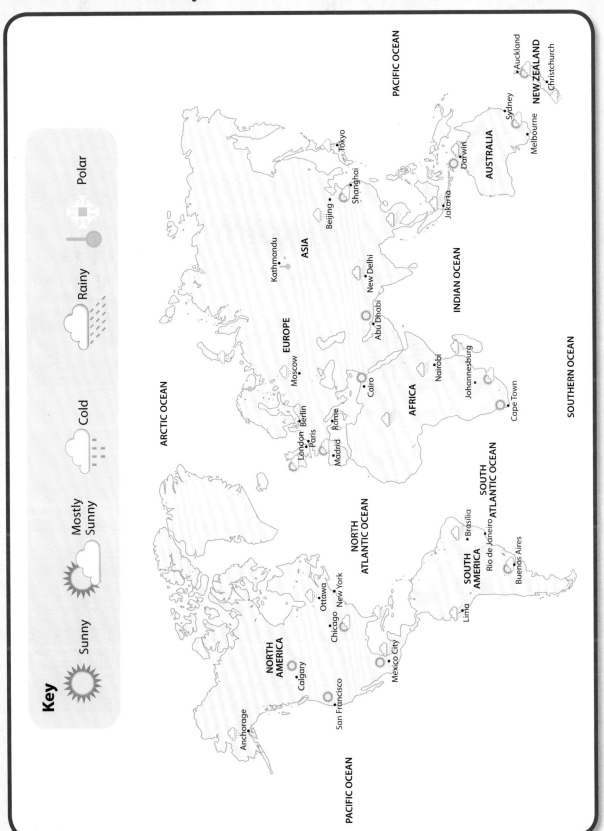

**Key**

| Sunny | Mostly Sunny | Cold | Rainy | Polar |

ARCTIC OCEAN

NORTH AMERICA

Anchorage
Calgary
San Francisco
Mexico City
Chicago
Ottawa
New York

PACIFIC OCEAN

NORTH ATLANTIC OCEAN

SOUTH AMERICA

Lima
Buenos Aires
Rio de Janeiro
Brasília

SOUTH ATLANTIC OCEAN

EUROPE

London
Paris
Berlin
Madrid
Rome
Moscow

ASIA

Kathmandu
Cairo
Abu Dhabi
New Delhi
Beijing
Shanghai
Tokyo

AFRICA

Nairobi
Johannesburg
Cape Town

INDIAN OCEAN

SOUTHERN OCEAN

Jakarta
Darwin

AUSTRALIA

Melbourne
Sydney

NEW ZEALAND

Auckland
Christchurch

PACIFIC OCEAN

▲ **This weather map shows what the weather is like all around the world.**

233

# No Key Needed: Picture Symbols

Most **maps** have a **key**. But there are some maps that don't have one. These maps use **symbols** that look like the real things they stand for.

Can you find the giraffes on this Picture Map?

# Picture Map

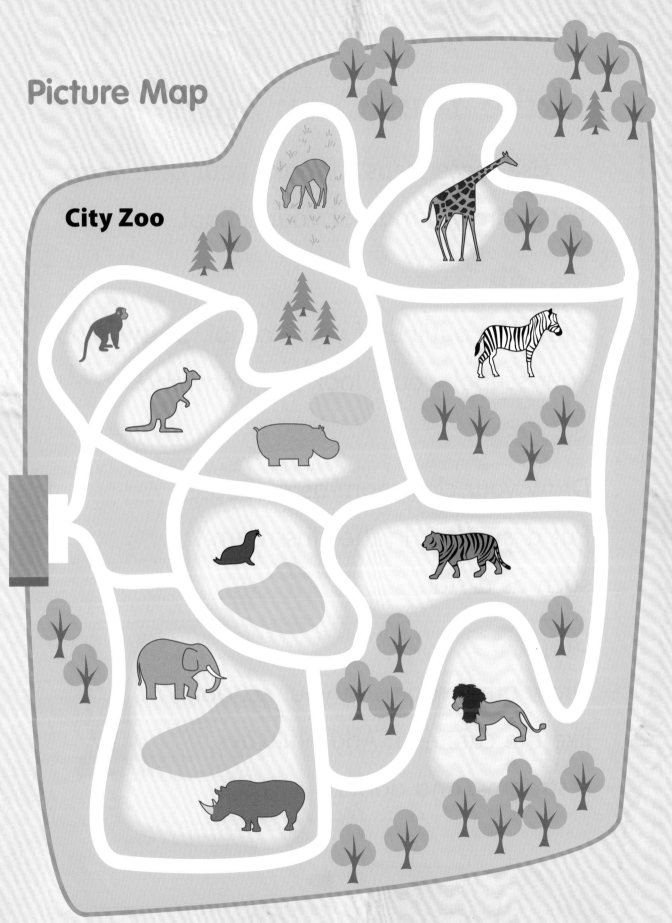

**City Zoo**

▲ This **picture map** uses picture **symbols** to show where to find the animals at the zoo.

# Make Your Own Map

Use these steps to make your own **map**. Try to draw a map of your school.

## Step 1

Draw the outline of your school. **Show** what your school would look like from above.

## Step 2

Draw your classroom as a square. Put a **symbol** in the classroom, such as a star.

## Step 3

Draw other rooms in your school, like the cafeteria. Add hallways, restrooms, and doors.

## Step **4**

Draw the library. Put a **symbol** in the library, such as an X.

## Step **5**

Make a **key** for your **map**. Draw and label the symbols for all the places you put on your map. ❖

## Picture Map

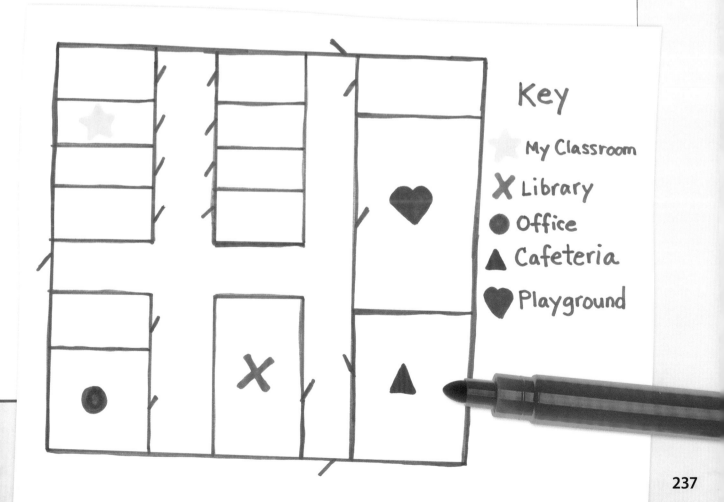

# Talk About It

1. What does a **map key show**?

   A map key shows _____ .

2. How is a weather map different than the other maps in the selection?

   A weather map _____ . The other maps _____ .

3. Why do people use road maps?

   People use road maps to _____ .

# Write About It

What did you learn from "If Maps Could Talk"? Write a comment.

I learned _____ from page _____ .

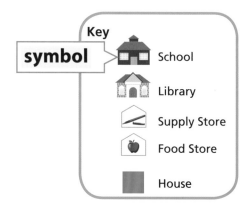

Key

symbol — School

Library

Supply Store

Food Store

House

# Use Information

What **signs** and **symbols** did you see in the text? What do they mean?

**T Chart**

| Symbols and Signs | What They Mean |
|---|---|
| | • mostly sunny<br>•<br>• |

Use your chart. Tell a partner what you learned about signs, symbols, and **maps**.

A symbol can be a **picture** of a real thing.

# Suffixes

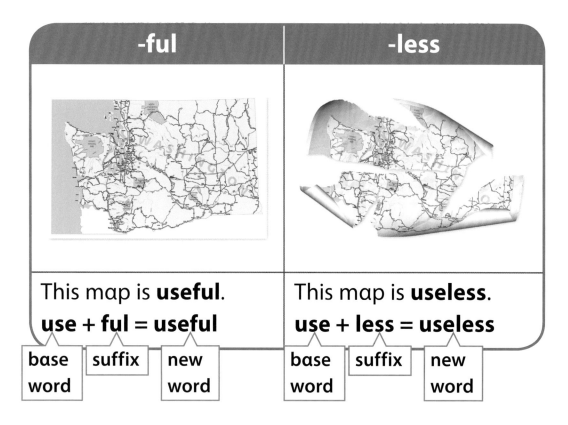

| -ful | -less |
|------|-------|
| This map is **useful**.<br>**use + ful = useful** | This map is **useless**.<br>**use + less = useless** |

base word · suffix · new word     base word · suffix · new word

Sometimes you can add a **suffix**, like **–ful** or **–less**, to the end of a word to make a new word. What do **useful** and **useless** mean?

Add **-ful** and **-less** to each word. How do the meanings change?

| Word | -ful | -less |
|------|------|-------|
| care | careful | careless |
| help | | |
| hope | | |

# Haiku

By Richard Wright

Keep straight down this block,
Then turn right where you will find
A peach tree blooming. ❖

# Compare Genres

How are the words in "If Maps Could Talk" and "Haiku" different?

**Informational Text**

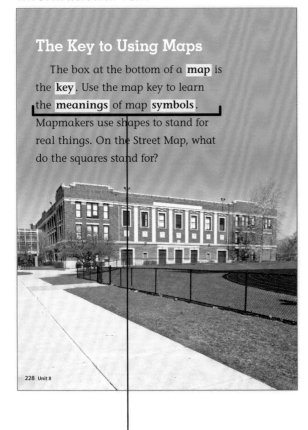

### The Key to Using Maps

The box at the bottom of a map is the key. Use the map key to learn the meanings of map symbols. Mapmakers use shapes to stand for real things. On the Street Map, what do the squares stand for?

228 Unit 8

The text gives definitions.

**Poem**

Keep straight down this block,
Then turn right where you will find
A peach tree blooming. ❖

242 Unit 8

The words create images in your mind.

**Talk Together**

Think about what you read and learned. Why do we need **maps**?

# Adverbs

An **adverb** can tell more about a **verb**.

We **stand** **quietly** by the peach tree.

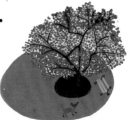

## Grammar Rules Adverbs

| Adverbs can tell: | Examples |
|---|---|
| • **how** something happens. These adverbs often end in -**ly**. | They **walk** **slowly**. |
| • **where** something happens. | The peach tree **is** **north** of the bench. |
| • **when** something happens. | We **always** **visit** the peach tree. |

## Read a Sentence

Which word is an adverb? How do you know?

The flower petals fall softly from the tree.

## Write a Sentence

Write a sentence to tell how you got ready for school today. Use an adverb.

**Chant**

## Tell a Story

Listen and chant.

# Jack and the Hike

A story has a problem,
A solution as well.
Here is an example
Of a story to tell.

Once upon a time,
A boy named Jack
Went on a hike
And lost his way back.

He looked to the east.
He looked to the west.
He looked for the path
That was the best.

He looked up and down,
And then . . . hooray!
He looked on a map
And found his way.

# 🔊 Key Words

lake

turn **right**

path

turn **left**

North

West

East

South

Jack's house

**Talk** **Together**

Use the map to tell a story.

# Identify Problem and Solution

**Problem-and-Solution Chart**

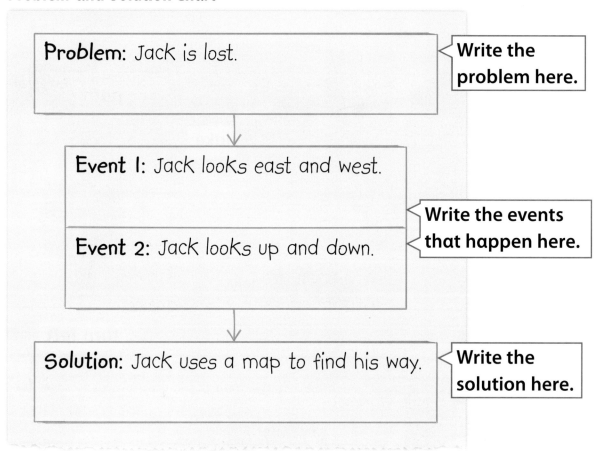

Problem: Jack is lost.  ⟵ **Write the problem here.**

↓

Event 1: Jack looks east and west.

Event 2: Jack looks up and down.  ⟵ **Write the events that happen here.**

↓

Solution: Jack uses a map to find his way.  ⟵ **Write the solution here.**

Look for problems and solutions as you listen or read.

**Talk Together**

Tell a different story. Imagine Jack is with a friend. Make a problem-and-solution chart.

## 🔊 More Key Words

### direction

North is a **direction**.

### • far

The red states are **far** from each other.

### • follow

path

**Follow** the path through the grass.

### location

our tent

Our tent is in a good **location** by the lake.

### • near

I sit **near** the window.

**Talk Together**

Describe a **Key Word** while your partner asks questions about it.

There are four of them. One of them is South.

Is it **direction**?

• Words to Know

# Vowel Sounds and Spellings: *ou, ow*

cloud

cow

**Listen** and **Learn**

Listen to each sentence. Choose the word that best finishes the sentence. Then write the word.

**1.** We walk on the _____ .

grind
ground
group

**2.** The king gets to wear a _____ .

crown
crust
crane

**3.** The _____ wants to eat some cheese.

miss
mouse
mince

**4.** The camel is _____ in color.

bran
brain
brown

🔊 Listen and read. Find the words with *ou* and *ow*.

## Using a Map

A map tells which way is north or south. It tells which way is east or west. A map helps you find your house. It helps you get around town.

It's good to learn how to use a map. One day, you might get lost. A map will help you go in the right direction. It will help you find your way home. Then, you can tell the story about how you found your way home.

**Work with a partner.**
Find the words with *ou* and *ow*. Sort the words into those with *ou* and those with *ow*. Then quiz each other on the words.

◀ Practice reading words with *ou* and *ow* by reading "Using a Map" with a partner.

# Read a Modern Fairy Tale

A **modern fairy tale** is a new version of an old story that has been told for many years.

| Most fairy tales begin like this. |

**Once upon a time**, a young girl lived in a village south of a forest.

## Reading Strategy

As you read, think of the 7 strategies you learned. Which strategies will help you understand the text?

# Little Red Riding Hood

by **Argentina Palacios**
illustrated by **Valeria Docompo**

Once upon a time, a young girl lived in a village **south** of a forest. She had a red riding hood. She loved it. She wore her red riding hood every day. So people called her Little Red Riding Hood.

One day, Little Red Riding Hood's mother said, "Grandma is sick. Take her some food. Visit with her for a while."

"Yes, Mom," Little Red Riding Hood said. "I will go now."

"**Follow** the shortest **path**. Do not get distracted. Go quickly!" her mother said. "Do not forget your map."

"Yes, Mom. I will take the map with me," said Little Red Riding Hood.

The village was **south** of the forest.
Grandma's house was **north** of the forest.
Little Red Riding Hood **followed** the
**directions** on her map. She knew exactly
where to go!

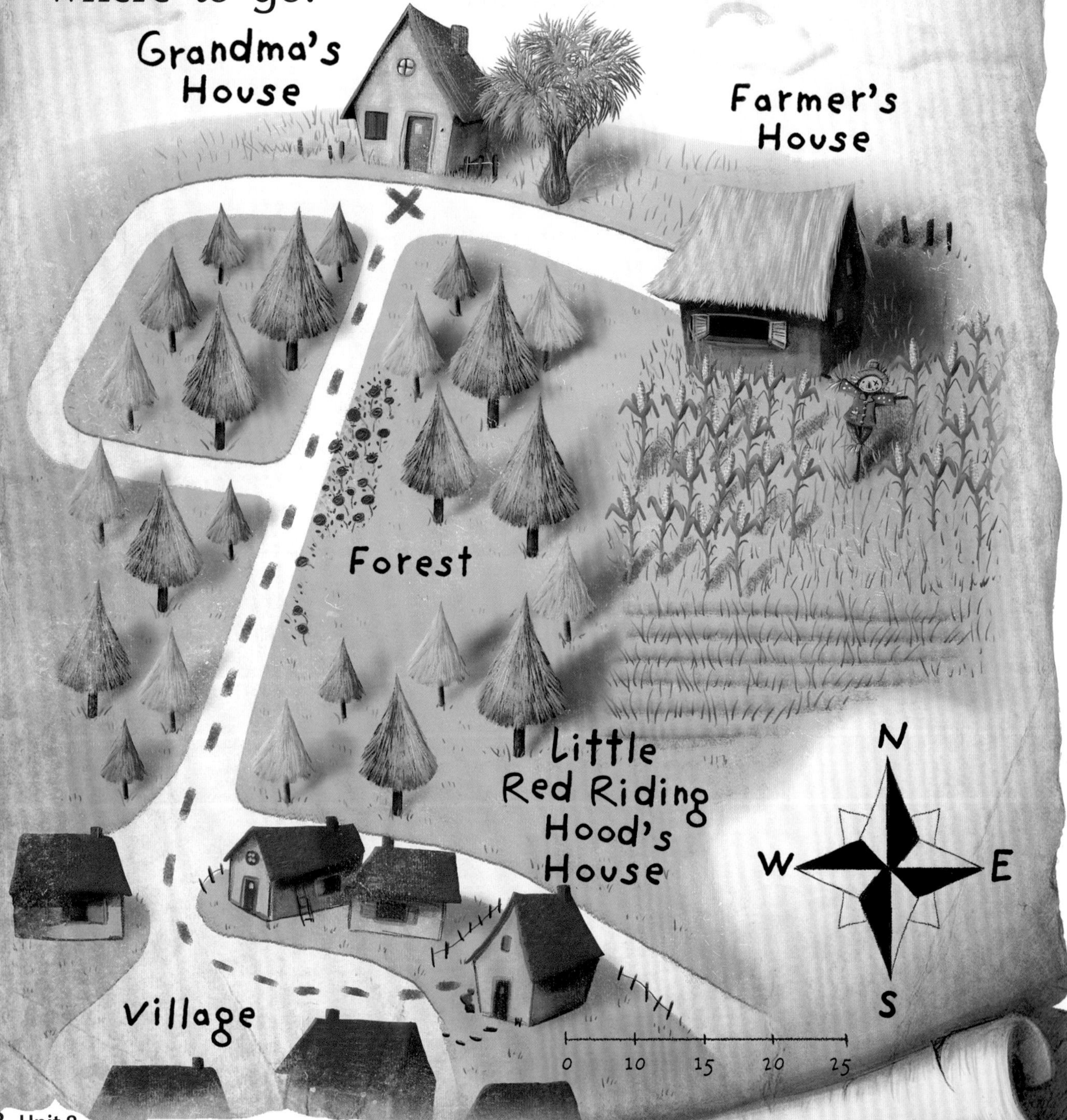

Grandma's
House

Farmer's
House

Forest

Little
Red Riding
Hood's
House

N

W          E

S

Village

0    10   15   20   25

Suddenly, a wolf stepped
out of the forest. He was big,
and he was bad. So people
called him Big Bad Wolf.

"Hello, Little Red Riding Hood,"
he said. "Look at those pretty
flowers. You should take some
flowers to your grandmother."

One, two, three, four flowers. Little Red
Riding Hood got distracted.

The wolf wanted to eat Little Red
Riding Hood. But people were walking on
the **path**. They would not want Little Red
Riding Hood to be eaten. They would
stop him.

Big Bad Wolf was unhappy. Then he had an idea.

He ran away, but Little Red Riding Hood didn't notice. She was too busy picking flowers for her grandmother.

Big Bad Wolf thought he could get to Grandma's house before Little Red Riding Hood. He checked his map to see what **path** he could take.

He ran to the **west**. Then he ran to the **north**. Then he ran a little to the **east**.

GRANDMA'S HOUSE

FARMER'S HOUSE

FOREST

LITTLE RED RIDING HOOD'S HOUSE

ILLAGE

263

Big Bad Wolf knocked on Grandma's door. "It is Little Red Riding Hood," he said.

"Come in, my dear," said Grandma.

The wolf looked at Grandma. He didn't want to eat her at all. She was too skinny.

"She does not look tasty," Big Bad Wolf said to himself. So he pushed Grandma out of the bed and into the closet!

Then Big Bad Wolf put on one of Grandma's nightgowns. "Now I look like Grandma. I will eat Little Red Riding Hood," he said to himself.

Little Red Riding Hood knocked on the door.

"Come in!" Big Bad Wolf tried to sound like Grandma. But his voice was too low.

"That does not sound like Grandma," Little Red Riding Hood said to herself. She opened the door. Something was wrong.

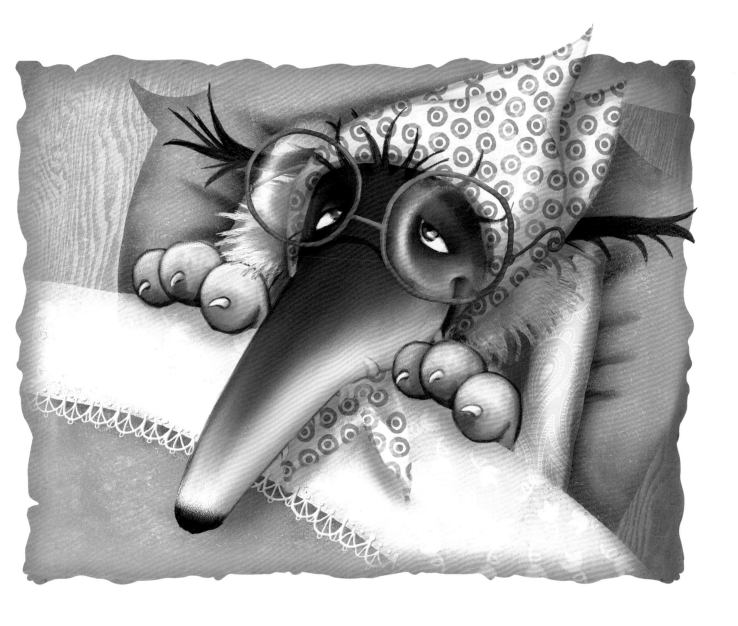

Little Red Riding Hood saw two
long ears. They were not Grandma's
ears.

Then she saw one very long nose.
It was not Grandma's nose.

She saw two little, brown eyes.
They were not Grandma's eyes.

Little Red Riding Hood thought fast. "Who can help me? The farmer can! I will go get the farmer!"

Little Red Riding Hood looked at her map. It showed where the farmer lived.

Grandma's House

Farmer's House

N
W        E
S

0    5    10    15    20

Little Red Riding Hood went **east**. She ran and ran. She told the farmer about the wolf.

"I scare rabbits out of my garden every day. I will scare away that wolf! I will save your Grandma!" he shouted. And they ran off together.

When Big Bad Wolf saw the angry
farmer, he jumped out of the bed. He
tried to go **right**. He tried to go **left**.
He could not escape. The farmer was
too fast for him. So Big Bad Wolf
jumped out of the window!

Little Red Riding Hood opened the
closet door. She helped her grandmother
back into the bed.

"Thank you for your help!" Little Red
Riding Hood said to the farmer. "I could
not have saved Grandma without you."

Grandma began to feel better quickly. She and the farmer became good friends. They never saw Big Bad Wolf again.

Little Red Riding Hood often came to visit her grandmother and the farmer. And they all lived happily ever after. ❖

## Meet the Author

# Argentina Palacios

**AWARD WINNER**

**Argentina Palacios** was born in Panama, and then moved to the United States. She was a Spanish teacher in Texas.

Now Ms. Palacios writes stories in English and Spanish. She also gives tours to children at a zoo because she loves animals.

**Writing Tip**

Argentina Palacios ended this story by solving the problem and telling us what happens to the characters afterward. What else would you add to the ending?

273

# Talk About It

**1.** Which character in the story is sick?

_____ is sick.

**2.** How does Big Bad Wolf get to Grandma's house before Little Red Riding Hood?

Big Bad Wolf _____ .

**3.** How does Little Red Riding Hood use a map to get help?

Little Red Riding Hood uses a map to _____ .

# Write About It

This fairy tale teaches you to know when you are in trouble and to go for help. When have you needed help? Who did you go to?

I needed help _____ .
I went to _____ .

# Identify Problem and Solution

Little Red Riding Hood has a problem with the Big Bad Wolf. What is it and how does she solve it?

**Problem-and-Solution Chart**

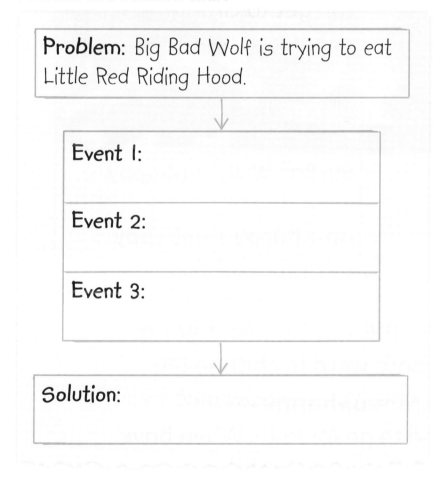

**Problem:** Big Bad Wolf is trying to eat Little Red Riding Hood.

Event 1:

Event 2:

Event 3:

Solution:

Use your chart to retell the story of "Little Red Riding Hood."

The farmer scares Big Bad Wolf away.

275

# Prefixes

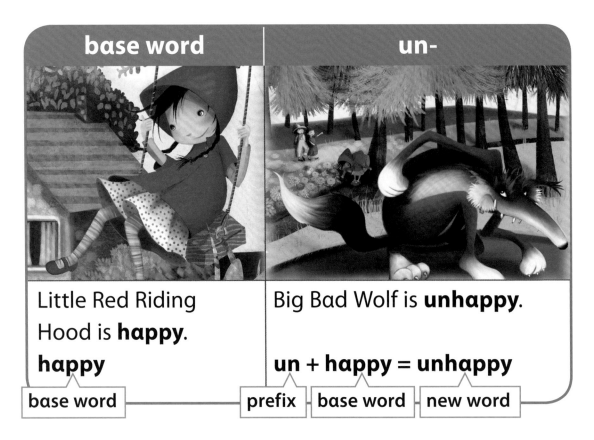

| base word | un- |
|---|---|
| Little Red Riding Hood is **happy**.<br><br>**happy**<br>base word | Big Bad Wolf is **unhappy**.<br><br>**un + happy = unhappy**<br>prefix · base word · new word |

A **prefix** is a word part. Add a prefix to the **beginning** of a base word to change the meaning. What does **unhappy** mean?

**Try It Together**

Add the prefix **un-** to each word. Talk about the new meaning of each word.

| Word | New Word |
|---|---|
| lucky | unlucky |
| safe | |
| kind | |
| fair | |

**Making Connections** Learn more about what helps us use maps.

**Genre** A **how-to article** teaches you how to do something.

# How to Make a Compass

## by Michael A. DiSpezio

A compass is a tool that can tell which **direction** you are going. There are four main directions: **North**, **South**, **East**, and **West**.

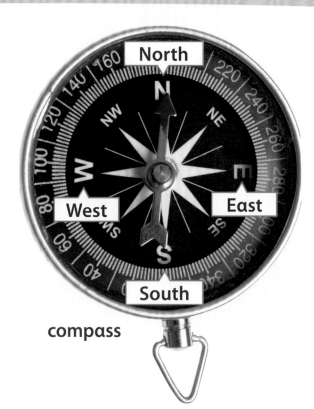

compass

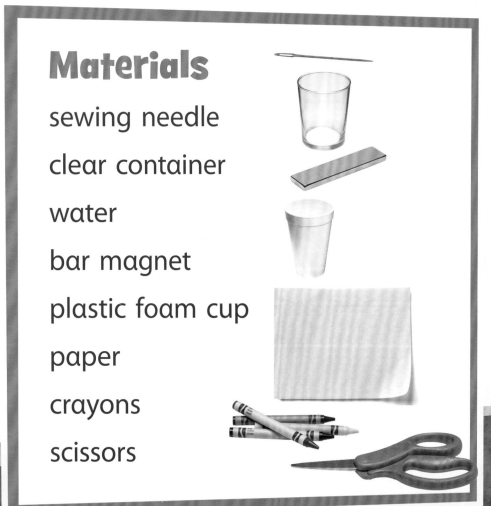

## Materials

sewing needle

clear container

water

bar magnet

plastic foam cup

paper

crayons

scissors

# Step 1

Cut out the bottom of the
foam cup so you have
a flat circle.

# Step 2

Magnetize the needle. Rub it the same
**direction** on the bar magnet 20 times.

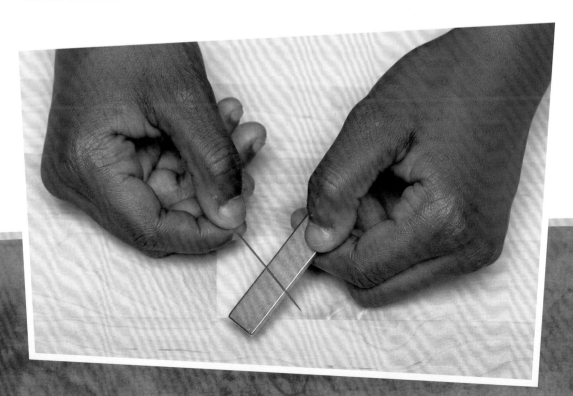

## Step 3

Lay the needle on the foam circle.

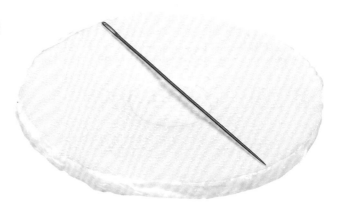

## Step 4

Put the foam and the needle in the water. The needle will stop moving when it points **North**.

# Step 5

Draw a compass rose like this one.

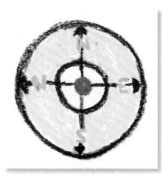

Fill the clear container with water. Place it over your compass rose.

# Step 6

Move the paper around until the needle lines up with the N on the compass rose.

Think of all the places **north** of you. Which places are **south** of you? ❖

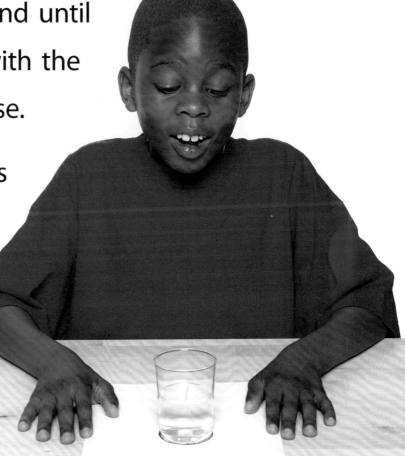

# Compare Genres

How are the purposes of a fairy tale like "Little Red Riding Hood" and a how-to article like "How to Make a Compass" different?

**Fairy Tale**

Suddenly, a wolf stepped out of the forest. He was big, and he was bad. So people called him Big Bad Wolf.

"Hello, Little Red Riding Hood," he said. "Look at those pretty flowers. You should take some flowers to your grandmother."

259

Tells a story that cannot happen in real life.

**How-to Article**

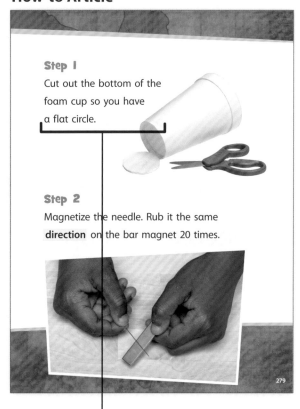

**Step 1**
Cut out the bottom of the foam cup so you have a flat circle.

**Step 2**
Magnetize the needle. Rub it the same **direction** on the bar magnet 20 times.

279

Tells how to make something that is real.

**Talk Together**

Think about what you read and learned. Why do we need maps?

# Prepositions

**Prepositions** tell where something is.

The needle is **on** the foam.

The cup is **next to** the scissors.

| **Grammar Rules** Prepositions | |
|---|---|
| Prepositions tell where. Put prepositions before the noun that names a place. | The compass is **on** the **table**. |

preposition

noun that names a place

## Read a Sentence

Draw what the sentence tells. Use your drawing to tell a partner what the preposition means.

The compass rose is **under** the glass.

## Write a Sentence

Write a sentence that tells where you find scissors in your classroom. Use a preposition. Read it to a partner.

# Write as a Reader

## Write Literary Response

Think about a story. What was the problem and solution? What did you like about it? Write a response for a partner.

Give the **title** of the story. **Underline** the title in your response.

Tell about the **solution** to the problem.

<u>Little Red Riding Hood</u>

by Aziza Noor

I read <u>Little Red Riding Hood</u>. Little Red Riding Hood had to save Grandma from the wolf.

Little Red Riding Hood ran to get the farmer. The helpful farmer scared the wolf away.

They all lived happily ever after. I think this happy ending makes <u>Little Red Riding Hood</u> a good story.

Describe the **problem**.

Tell **what you liked** about the story.

**1** **Plan and Write**

Talk with a partner about stories
you have read. Pick one story
you like. Talk about how the author tells the story.
Tell your partner the story's problem and solution.

Write the problem and solution. Then write what
makes the story good.

**2** **Check Your Work**

Revise and edit your writing.
Use this checklist.

**3** **Finish and Share**

Finish your response. Write
each sentence neatly. Begin
a new paragraph when you
change ideas.

Read your response clearly.
Listen carefully to your
partner. Then ask questions.
Share what you know.

**Checklist**

☑ Does the story you reviewed have a strong ending?

☑ Can you add any prefixes or suffixes?

☑ Check your sentences. Did you use prepositions correctly?

☑ Check for different ways to spell sounds you know. Circle words to check. Correct spelling errors.

Why was the ending your favorite part of "Little Red Riding Hood"?

Why do we need maps?

## Share Your Ideas

Think about what maps show us. Why do we need maps? Choose one of these ways to share your ideas about the **Big Question**.

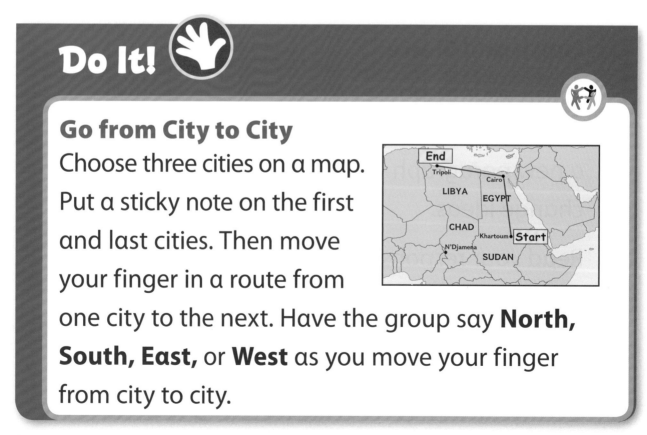

### Do It!

**Go from City to City**
Choose three cities on a map. Put a sticky note on the first and last cities. Then move your finger in a route from one city to the next. Have the group say **North, South, East,** or **West** as you move your finger from city to city.

End
Tripoli
Cairo
LIBYA
EGYPT
CHAD
Khartoum **Start**
N'Djamena
SUDAN

# Talk About It!

### Give Directions
Hide an object, such as a crayon. Then give good directions so that your partner can find the object. Take turns.

> Go to the plants near the window. Look between the books.

# Write It!

### Draw a Map
Draw a map of your neighborhood. Use symbols in your map. Draw a map key that shows what the symbols stand for.

My Neighborhood

Spring Street

Key
House
Park

# Picture Dictionary

The definitions are for the words as they are introduced in the selections of this book.

## Parts of an Entry

The **entry** shows how the word is spelled.

The **picture** helps you understand more about the meaning of the word.

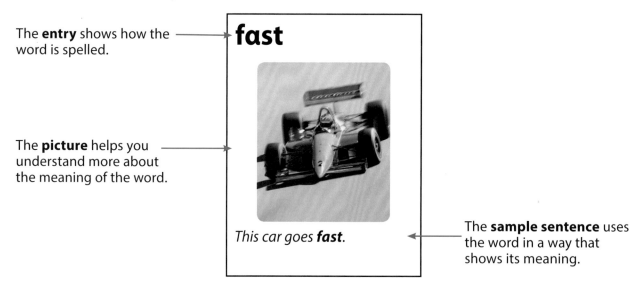

**fast**

*This car goes **fast**.*

The **sample sentence** uses the word in a way that shows its meaning.

## A

## alike

*These cats are **alike**.*

## B

## back

*The **back** tire is flat.*

## beak

*This bird's **beak** is colorful.*

## better

*Martha got a **better** grade.*

## between

*The house is **between** the two trees.*

## blow

*The wind will **blow** the tree down.*

# body

*A baby has a small **body**.*

# build

*You can **build** things with blocks.*

**C**

# calendar

*This **calendar** shows the month of December.*

# climb

*Orangutans can **climb** trees.*

# cloudy

*It is a **cloudy** day.*

# cold

*It's **cold** today.*

# communicate

*People **communicate** by talking and writing.*

# computer

*Jim does work on a **computer**.*

# cool

*The fan keeps me **cool**.*

# corner

Ashley Miller

*I write my name in the **corner** of the paper.*

# coverings

feathers

shell

*Birds and turtles have different **coverings**.*

## different

*These fruits are **different**.*

## direction

*North is a **direction**.*

## distance

*This man runs a long **distance**.*

## easier

*It is **easier** to carry the books one at a time.*

## east

New York

*New York is on the **east** coast of the United States.*

## fact

*It's a **fact** that a dog has four legs.*

# far

*The red states are **far** from each other.*

# fast

*This car goes **fast**.*

# feathers

*This eagle's **feathers** help it to fly.*

# feature

*A long neck is the main **feature** of a giraffe.*

# feel

*The rabbit's fur **feels** soft.*

# fly

*The gulls **fly** together.*

# follow

path

**Follow** the path through the grass.

# front

The **front** of the house is blue.

# fur

This big dog has a lot of **fur**.

# future

| past | present | future |
|------|---------|--------|
| kindergarten | first grade | second grade |

In the **future**, I will be in second grade.

H

# history

Study **history** to learn what happened long ago.

# hot

The stove is **hot**.

# Internet

*Sarah reads good news on the **Internet**.*

# invent

*People **invent** things like the telephone.*

# key

*A map **key** uses symbols to show where things are.*

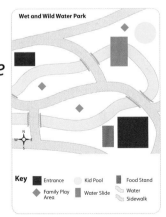

# left

*Turn **left** when you see this sign.*

# location

*Our tent is in a good **location** by the lake.*

# look

*These apples **look** the same.*

a
b
c
d
e
f
g
h
i
j
k
l
**m**
n
o
p
q
r
s
t
u
v
w
x
y
z

## machine

*This **machine** washes dishes.*

## map

*This **map** shows where they are.*

## meaning

*The dictionary shows us the **meaning** of words.*

## message

*Jane got a text **message**.*

## modern

*The cell phone is more **modern** than the old phone.*

## month

*Our favorite **month** is July.*

# mouth

This alligator has a large **mouth**.

# movement

The **movement** of a tortoise is slow.

# music

This **music** is very loud.

# near

I sit **near** the window.

# new

This family has a **new** baby.

# news

He is watching the **news** on TV.

# north

*Nebraska is **north** of Texas.*

# now

*The test starts right **now**.*

**O**

# old

*This car is very **old**.*

# outside

*They run **outside**.*

**P**

# parts

*This engine has many **parts**.*

# past

| past | present | future |
|------|---------|--------|
| kindergarten | first grade | second grade |

*In the **past**, I was in kindergarten.*

# path

This **path** goes through the woods.

# paw

This is a cat's **paw**.

# picture

These **pictures** sit on a desk.

# power

This toaster uses **power**.

# present

| past | present | future |
|------|---------|--------|
| kindergarten | first grade | second grade |

Today is the **present**. I am in first grade.

# push

We had to **push** the car.

a b c d e f g h i j k l m n o p q **r** **s** t u v w x y z

## R

### rainy

*It is a **rainy** day.*

### record

*This old **record** has some fun music.*

### right

*Turn **right** when you see this sign.*

### run

*We like to **run**.*

## S

### scales

*The **scales** on this snake are beautiful.*

### show

*I **show** my drawing.*

# sign

*This **sign** means "do not."*

# snowy

*This mountain is very **snowy**.*

# slide

*We like to **slide** at the park.*

# soft

pillow

*Pillows are **soft**.*

# slither

*The snake **slithers** across the ground.*

# south

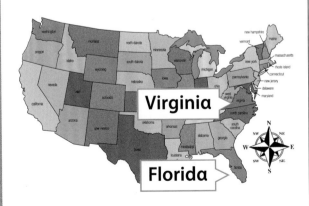

Virginia

Florida

*Florida is **south** of Virginia.*

# storm

Our family stays inside when there is a **storm**.

# strong

We are **strong**.

# sunny

It is a **sunny** day.

# swim

We like to **swim** in the pool.

# symbol

This flag is a **symbol** of America.

**T**

# tail

This lemur has a long **tail**.

## temperature

*The **temperature** is 8° Fahrenheit.*

## then

*Back **then**, I didn't know how to walk.*

## tool

*A dictionary is a **tool** you can use to look up words.*

## useful

*This hammer is very **useful**.*

## warm

*The blanket keeps us **warm**.*

## weather

*We like the warm **weather**.*

## west

California

*California is on the **west** coast of the United States.*

## wind

*The **wind** is very strong today.*

Y

## year

*This has been a fun **year**.*

# Index

**Content vocabulary**

*see Vocabulary*

**Context clues**

unfamiliar words 213

using to determine meanings 213

**Conventions**, in writing

capitalization

for months and days of week 213

for proper nouns 213

for salutation and closing of letter 213

to begin sentences 41

parts of speech

adverbs 245

nouns 283

prepositions 283, 285

verbs 69, 181, 211, 213, 245

punctuation

to end sentences 41, 71, 109, 141, 143

**Creative projects** 3, 43, 44, 71, 72, 73, 75, 102, 144, 145, 147, 213, 214, 217, 220, 286, 287

**Critical thinking** 32, 62, 100, 134, 172, 202, 238, 274

**D**

**Describe**

actions **184**, **203**

people and things 31, 70, 144, 145, **184**, **203**, 212, 214, 249

**Details**

locating 44, **63**, 70, 82, 112, 116, 134, **135**, 150, **173**, 202

identifying 44, **63**, 70, 71, 82, 112, 116, 134, **135**, 150, **173**, 202, 212, 213

about stories **63**, 82, 116, 134, **135**, 150, **173**, 202

**Determine importance**

main idea and details 44, 63, 70, 71, 82, 112, 135, **150**, **173**, 202, **212**, 213, 224, 252

summarize **63**

**Dictionary**

definitions in **174**, **204**

using **174**, **204**

**Directions** 217, 218, 219, 241, 247, 286, 287

following **218**, 219, 247, 286, 287

**E**

**End marks** **41**, 71, **109**, 141, 143

**Explain** 76, 77, 78, 100, **101**, 142, 143, 145, 181, 211

**Express feelings** **182**, 183, 184, 213, 214

**Express ideas** 6, 32, 36, 40, 44, 62, 64, 68, 71, 73, **76**, 77, 78, 100, 102, 108, 111, 112, 134, 136, 140, 143, 147, 170, 174, 180, 184, 203, 210, 213, 214, 217, 220, 238, 240, 244, 248, 274, 276, 282, 285

# T

**Tell a story** **246**, 247, 248

**Text features**

illustrations 10, 82, 85, 86, 87, 88, 89, 90–91, 92, 93, 94, 96, 97, 98–99

labels 46, 50, 52, 53, 54, 55, 56, 57, 58, 59, 60

maps **224**, 227, 229, 231, 233, 235, 237

timeline 154, 170–171

**Then and now** 146, 147, 148, 149, 155–171, 173, 175–179, 180, 182, 183, 210, 212, 213, 214, 215

**Timeline** 154, 170–171

**Topic**

main idea and 44, 63, 70, 71, 82, 112, 135, 150, 173, 212, 213

# U

**Unfamiliar words**

*see Context clues; Dictionary*

**Use information** **220**, **239**

# V

**Venn Diagram** 6, 33, 44, 78, 112, 150, 180, 184, 220, 248

**Verbs** 69, **181**, 201, 213, **245**

*see also Adverbs; Conventions; Future tense verbs; Irregular verbs; Past tense verbs; Regular verbs; Subject-verb agreement*

**Visualize** **154**, **188**, 224, 252

**Vocabulary**

academic 7, 45, 79, 113, 151, 185, 214, 221, 249

science 5, 43, 77, 111

social studies 149, 183, 214, 219, 247

strategies

ask questions 45, 113, 221, 249

count syllables 79

describe words 249

draw pictures 185

make flashcards 151

sort words 79

use a dictionary 174, 204

use words in context 7, 151, 214

words to know 7, 45, 79, 221, 249

# W

**Weather** 74, 75, 76, 77, 78, 108, 110, 111, 112, 134, 135, 140, 142, 143, 144, 145

*see also Storms; Wind*

**Wind** 83–99, 103–107

**Words to know** 4, 7, 33, 42, 76, 79, 110, 148, 182, 218, 221, 246, 249

**Writing**

paragraphs **142**, 285

sentences

# Index of Authors

# Index of Illustrators

## Text and Illustrator Credits

### Unit Five

**Houghton Mifflin Harcourt Company:** Text and illustrations from *For Pete's Sake* by Ellen Stoll Walsh. Copyright © 1998 by Ellen Stoll Walsh. Reprinted by permission of Houghton Mifflin Harcourt Publishing Company. All rights reserved.

**School Specialty Publishing:** Excerpt from *Slither, Slide, Hop and Run* by Katharine Kenah. Published in 2006 by School Specialty Publishing.

### Unit Six

**HarperCollins Publisher:** Excerpt from *I Face the Wind* by Vicki Cobb, illustrated by Julia Gorton. Text copyright © 2003 Vicki Cobb, illustrations copyright © 2003 Julia Gorton. Used by permission of HarperCollins Publishers and Susan Schulman Literary Agency.

**Houghton Mifflin Harcourt Company:** Text and illustrations from *A Year for Kiko* by Ferida Wolff, illustrated by Joung Un Kim. Text copyright © 1997 by Ferida Wolff. Illustrations copyright © 1997 by Joung Un Kim. Used by permission of Houghton Mifflin Harcourt Publishing Company and Ferida Wolff. All rights reserved.

### Unit Seven

**Lerner Publishing Group:** Excerpt from *Communication Then and Now* by Robin Nelson. Published in 2003 by Lerner Publishing Group, Inc.

### Unit Eight

**Capstone Press:** Excerpted from the work entitled *If Maps Could Talk: Using Symbols and Keys* by Erika L. Shores © 2008 by Capstone Press. All rights reserved.

**Arcade Publishing:** "Keep straight down this block," by Richard Wright, from *Haiku: This Other World.* Copyright © 1999 by Ellen Wright. Published by Arcade Publishing, an imprint of Skyhorse Publishing. Reprinted by permission of the publisher.

## Photographic Credits

Cover Chue Ardi. iii (tl) kuritafsheen/Getty Images. (tr) Jim Reed/National Geographic Image Collection. (bl) Ami Vitale. (br) KidStock/Getty Images. v Zview/E+/Getty Images. xi eldirector77/Shutterstock.com. 2–3 kuritafsheen/Getty Images. 3 Liz Garza Williams/Hampton-Brown/National Geographic School Publishing. 4 JAD DAVENPORT/National Geographic Image Collection. 5 (tl) cyo bo/Shutterstock.com. (tr) Michael Lynch/Shutterstock.com. (cl) Eric Isselee/Shutterstock.com. (cr) Eric Isselee/Shutterstock.com. (bl) Yuri Kevhiev/Alamy Stock Photo. (br) mai111/Shutterstock.com. 6 (tl) Jello5700/Getty Images. (tr) Edwin Verin/Shutterstock.com. (bl) THEPALMER/E+/Getty Images. (br) Steve Allen/Stockbyte/Getty Images. 7 (tl) otsphoto/Shutterstock.com. (tc) ideabug/Getty Images. (tr-apple) iStock.com/Dimitris66. (tr-banana) jamakosy/Shutterstock.com. (bl) davegkugler/Shutterstock.com. (bc) iStock.com/Dimitris66. 8 (tl) DnD-Production.com/Shutterstock.com. (tr) Le Panda/Shutterstock.com. (bl) Kalidron.Photography/Shutterstock.com. (br) hxdbzxy/Shutterstock.com. 9 Laura Leyshon/Moment Open/Getty Images. 32 Robert Kneschke/Shutterstock.com. 33 StevieS/Getty Images. 35 Heidi & Hans-Juergen Koch/Minden Pictures/Superstock. 36 Otis Imboden/National Geographic Image Collection. 37 Kevin Schafer/Alamy Stock Photo. 38–39 Zview/E+/Getty Images. 40 Otis Imboden/National Geographic Image Collection. 41 GlobalP/iStock/

Getty Images. 42 Ljupco/Getty Images. 43 (tl) stephan kerkhofs/Shutterstock.com. (tr) Tom Brakefield/Stockbyte/Getty Images. (cl) Ondrej Prosicky/Shutterstock.com. (cr) Luiz Claudio Marigo/Nature Picture Library. (bl) sirtravelalot/Shutterstock.com. (br) Frans Lemmens/Corbis Unreleased/Getty Images. 44 (l) Abramova Kseniya/Shutterstock.com. (r) Andreas Weiss/Shutterstock.com. 45 (tl) Nick Kirk/Alamy Stock Photo. (tc) SednevaAnna/Getty Images. (tr) colin streater/Alamy Stock Photo. (bl) Chris Mattison/age fotostock/Shutterstock.com. (bc) Piotr Sikora/Shutterstock.com. 46 (l) 3Dalia/Shutterstock.com. (c) Maciej Es/Shutterstock.com. (r) MRB photography/Shutterstock.com. 47 Lhadpo/Shutterstock.com. 48 BirdImages/Getty Images. 48–49 Rich Lindie/iStock/Getty Images. 50 (t) BirdImages/Getty Images. (b) Paul Tessier/Shutterstock.com. 51 (t) fivespots/Shutterstock.com. (b) Paul Chesley/Stone/Getty Images. 52 (t) Eric Isselee/Shutterstock.com. (b)John Carnemolla/iStock/Getty Images. 53 Melory/Shutterstock.com. 54 (t) pkruger/iStock/Getty Images. (b) mattabbe/iStock/Getty Images. 55 EcoPrint/Shutterstock.com. 56 Eric Isselee/Shutterstock.com. 57 Wojciech Jaskowski/Shutterstock.com. 58 H Lansdown/Alamy Stock Photo. 59 Edd Westmacott./Alamy Stock Photo. 60 (t) Eric Isselee/Shutterstock.com. (b) x-posure/Getty Images. 61 (t) waynetam/iStock/Getty Images. (b) Ingram Publishing/Alamy Stock Photo. 63 MichaelDeLeon/E+/Getty Images. 64 (l) Eric Isselee/Shutterstock.com. (r) pkruger/iStock/Getty Images. 65 (l) Greg Marshall/National Geographic Image Collection. (r) You Touch Pix of EuToch/Shutterstock.com. 66 (t) Mark Mallchok/Brella Productions. (b) Dr. Michael Heithaus. 67 (t. b) Greg Marshall/National Geographic Image Collection. 68 (tl) pkruger/iStock/Getty Images. (bl) mattabbe/iStock/Getty Images. (tr) Mark Mallchok/Brella Productions. (br) Dr. Michael Heithaus. 69 spxChrome/E+/Getty Images. 71 Liz Garza Williams/Hampton-Brown/National Geographic School Publishing. 72 kuritafsheen/Getty Images. 73 (l) Ariel Skelley/DigitalVision/Getty Images. (r) Jose Luis Pelaez Inc/Blend Images/Getty Images. 74–75 Jim Reed/National Geographic Image Collection. 75 Liz Garza Williams/Hampton-Brown/National Geographic School Publishing. 76 Terry Vine/Getty Images. 77 (tl) Zastolskiy Victor/Shutterstock.com. (tr) cristovao/Shutterstock.com. (bl) Michael Rolands/Shutterstock.com. (br) ND1939/iStock/Getty Images. 78 whiran/Shutterstock.com. 79 (tl) David Madison/Photodisc/Getty Images. (tc) Jupiterimages/Polka Dot/Getty Images. (tr) Design Pics Inc/Alamy Stock Photo. (bl) Nicholas Eveleigh/Alamy Stock Photo. (bc) Jim Arbogast/DigitalVision/Getty Images. 80 (l) Lee M Atwater/Shutterstock.com. (r) Lakeview Images/Shutterstock.com. 81 Lester Balajadia/Shutterstock.com. 101 (l) nicolesy/iStock/Getty Images. (r) JohnnyGreig/E+/Getty Images. 111 (tl) XiXinXing/Shutterstock.com. (tr) Randy Faris/Corbis/VCG/Getty images. (cl) Antonio Jorge Nunes/Shutterstock.com. (cr) Sam Abell/National Geographic Image Collection. (b) titoOnz/Shutterstock.com. 112 Anna Grigorjeva/Shutterstock.com. 113 (tl) George F. Mobley/National Geographic Image Collection. (tc) Nick Kennedy/Alamy Stock Photo. (tr) Masterfile. (bl) NoDerog/Getty Images. (bc) skodonnell/iStock/Getty Images. 114 (tl) Siyapath/Shutterstock.com. (tc) TobiasD/Shutterstock.com. (tr) Dirk Jonker/Shutterstock.com. (cl) Real PIX/Shutterstock.com. (cr) JoeSAPhotos/Shutterstock.com. (bl) Igor Kruglikov/Shutterstock.com. (br) zulfachri zulkifli/Shutterstock.com. 115 Kokhanchikov/Shutterstock.com. 133 Ferida Wolff. 135 Andersen Ross/Getty Images. 137 Carsten Peter/National Geographic Image Collection. 138 (tc) Rebecca Hale/National Geographic Image Collection. (cl) Warren Faidley/

Corbis/Getty Images. 138–139 Carsten Peter/National Geographic Image Collection. 140 Carsten Peter/National Geographic Image Collection. 141 (t) Rebecca Hale/National Geographic Image Collection. (b) Siede Preis/Stockbyte/Getty Images. 144 Jim Reed/National Geographic Image Collection. 145 (t) Jose Luis Pelaez Inc/Blend Images/Getty Images. (b) Rick Holcomb/Hampton-Brown/National Geographic School Publishing. 146–147 Ami Vitale. 147 Jupiterimages/PHOTOS.com/Getty Images. 148 Clover No.7 Photography/Getty Images. 149 (tl) George Marks/Retrofile RF/Getty Images. (tr) princessdlaf/iStock/Getty Images. (cl) George Marks/Hulton Archive/Getty Images. (cr) peepo/E+/Getty Images. (bl) George Marks/Retrofile RF/Getty Images. (br) Cultura Motion/Shutterstock.com. 150 SOURCENEXT/Alamy Stock Photo. 151 (bl) VaLiza/Shutterstock.com. (br) Bettmann/Getty Images. (tr) Tom Clausen/Shutterstock.com. 152 (tl) Potapov Alexander/Shutterstock.com. (cl) OlesyaNickolaeva/Shutterstock.com. (cr) Andrey Armyagov/Shutterstock.com. (bl) Syda Productions/Shutterstock.com. (br) Jeffry Surianto/Shutterstock.com. 153 scanrail/Getty Images. 154 (tl) Science & Society Picture Library/Getty Images. (tc) World History Archive/Alamy Stock Photo. (tr) Science & Society Picture Library/Getty Images. (bl) North Wind Picture Archives/Alamy Stock Photo. (br) Science & Society Picture Library/Getty Images. 155 (t) Minnesota Historical Society/Getty Images. (b) ferrantraite/E+/Getty Images. 156–157 Blend Images/Superstock. 158 Pierre Vauthey/Sygma/Sygma via Getty Images. 159 funstock/Getty Images. 160 (t) The Granger Collection. New York. (b) EmiSta/Getty Images. 161 Lester Lefkowitz/Getty Images. (inset) Giakita/Shutterstock.com. 162 (t) Fotosearch/Archive Photos/Getty Images. (b) Adrio/iStock/Getty Images. 163 SYUJI NISHIDA/amana images/Getty Images. (inset) Bettmann/Getty Images. 164 (t) Underwood Archives/Archive Photos/Getty Images. (b) cyphix-photo/Shutterstock.com. 165 JGI/Tom Grill/Blend Images/Getty Images. (inset) Elly Godfroy/Alamy Stock Photo. 166 Library of Congress. Prints & Photographs Division. Reproduction number LC-USZ62-76951 (b&w film copy neg.). (inset) Old Paper Studios/Alamy Stock Photo. 167 (t) David Young-Wolff/PhotoEdit. (b) sjlocke/Deposit Photos. 168 FPG/Retrofile RF/Getty Images. 169 Rawpixel/Shutterstock.com. 170 (tl) Science & Society Picture Library/Getty Images. (tr) World History Archive/Alamy Stock Photo. (bl) North Wind Picture Archives/Alamy Stock Photo. (br) Science & Society Picture Library/Getty Images. 171 (tl) Science & Society Picture Library/Getty Images. (tr) SSPL/The Image Works. (bl) Keystone-France/Getty Images. (br) mikeledray/Shutterstock.com. 172 (l) Liz Garza Williams/Hampton-Brown/National Geographic School Publishing. (r) InesBazdar/Shutterstock.com. 173 (l) 3bugsmom/iStock/Getty Images. (r) Svitlana-ua/Shutterstock.com. 174 (l) Monkey Business Images/Stockbroker/Getty Images. (r) PeopleImages/E+/Getty Images. 175 (bg) Triff/Shutterstock.com. (inset) Tomasz Szymanski/Shutterstock.com. 176 NG Images/Alamy Stock Photo. 176–177 Triff/Shutterstock.com. 177 Stocktrek/Getty Images. 178 NASA Photo/Alamy Stock Photo. 178–179 Triff/Shutterstock.com. 179 NASA. 184 Liz Garza Williams/Hampton-Brown/National Geographic School Publishing. 185 (tl) Asia Images Group Pte Ltd/Alamy Stock Photo. (tc) Holly Kuchera/Dreamstime.com. (tr) Irina Drazowa-fischer/Dreamstime.com. (bl) scanrail/Getty Images. (bc) W. Scott McGill/Shutterstock.com. (br) Sebastian Crocker/Shutterstock.com. (c) Jaletan/Shutterstock.com. 186 (l) MIA Studio/Shutterstock.com. (r) Billion Photos/Shutterstock.com. 187 Jenson/Shutterstock.com. 201 Marvin Lee. 202 (t) Kamyshko/Shutterstock.com. (c) Elenathewise/

# Acknowledgments

The Authors and Publisher would like to thank the following reviewers and teaching professionals for their valuable feedback during the development of the series.

**Literature Reviewers**

Carmen Agra Deedy, Grace Lin, Jonda C. McNair, Anastasia Suen

**Global Reviewers**

**USA/Canada:**

**Kristin Blathras,** Lead Literacy Teacher, Donald Morrill Elementary School, Chicago, IL; **Anna Ciani,** ESL Teacher, PS 291, Bronx, NY; **Jonathan Eversoll,** International Baccalaureate Curriculum Coach, Park Center Senior High, Brooklyn Park, MN; **Barbara A. Genovese-Fraracci,** District Program Specialist, Hacienda La Puente Unified School District, Hacienda Heights, CA; **Vanessa Gonzalez,** ESL Teacher/ESL Specialist, Rhoads Elementary, Katy, TX; **Leonila Izaguirre,** Bilingual-ESL Director, Pharr-San Juan-Alamo Independent School District, Pharr, TX; **Myra Junyk,** Literacy Consultant, Toronto, ON; **Susan Mayberger,** Coordinator of ESL, Migrant and Refugee Education, Omaha Public Schools, Omaha, NE; **Stephanie Savage Cantu,** Bilingual Teacher, Stonewall Jackson Elementary School, Dallas, TX; **Annette Torres Elias,** Consultant, Plano, TX; **Sonia James Upton,** ELL Consultant, Title III, Kentucky Department of Education, Frankfort, KY

**Asia:**

**Mohan Aiyer,** School Principal, Brainworks International School, Yangon; **Andrew Chuang,** Weige Primary School, Taipei; **Sherefa Dickson,** Head Teacher, SMIC, Beijing; **Ms Hien,** IP Manager, IPS Vietnam, Ho Chi Minh; **Christine Huang,** Principal, The International Bilingual School at the Hsinchu Science Park (IBSH), Hsinchu; **Julie Hwang,** Academic Consultant, Seoul; **David Kwok,** CEO, Englit Enterprise, Guangzhou; **Emily Li,** Teaching Assistant, SMIC, Beijing; **Warren Martin,** English Teacher, Houhai English, Beijing; **Bongse Memba,** Academic Coordinator, SMIC, Beijing; **Hoai Minh Nguyen,** Wellspring International Bilingual School, Ho Chi Minh; **Mark Robertson,** Elementary School Principal, Yangon Academy, Yangon; **Daphne Tseng,** American Eagle Institute, Hsinchu; **Amanda Xu,** Director of Teaching and Research, Englit Enterprise, Guangzhou; **Alice Yamamoto,** ALT, PL Gakuen Elementary School, Osaka; **Yan Yang,** Director of Research Development, Houhai English, Beijing

**Middle East:**

**Lisa Olsen,** Teacher, GEMS World Academy, Dubai, United Arab Emirates; **Erin Witthoft,** Curriculum Coordinator, Universal American School, Kuwait

**Latin America:**

**Federico Brull,** Academic Director, Cambridge School of Monterrey, Mexico; **Elizabeth Caballero,** English Coordinator, Ramiro Kolbe Campus Otay, Mexico; **Renata Callipo,** Teacher, CEI Romualdo, Brazil; **Lilia Huerta,** General Supervisor, Ramiro Kolbe Campus Presidentes, Mexico; **Rosalba Millán,** English Coordinator Primary, Instituto Cenca, Mexico; **Ann Marie Moreira,** Academic Consultant, Brazil; **Raúl Rivera,** English Coordinator, Ramiro Kolbe Campus Santa Fe, Mexico; **Leonardo Xavier,** Teacher, CEI Romualdo, Brazil

The Publisher gratefully acknowledges the contributions of the following National Geographic Explorers to our program and planet:

Greg Marshall and Tim Samaras